BRIGHT NOTES

THE PHILOSOPHY OF ST. THOMAS AQUINAS

Intelligent Education

Nashville, Tennessee

BRIGHT NOTES: The Philosophy of St. Thomas Aquinas
www.BrightNotes.com

No part of this publication may be used or reproduced in any manner whatsoever without written permission, except in the case of brief quotations in critical articles and reviews. For permissions, contact Influence Publishers http://www.influencepublishers.com.

ISBN: 978-1-645424-38-3 (Paperback)
ISBN: 978-1-645424-39-0 (eBook)

Published in accordance with the U.S. Copyright Office Orphan Works and Mass Digitization report of the register of copyrights, June 2015.

Originally published by Monarch Press.
Gerard J. Dalcourt, 1965
2020 Edition published by Influence Publishers.

Interior design by Lapiz Digital Services. Cover Design by Thinkpen Designs.

Printed in the United States of America.

Library of Congress Cataloging-in-Publication Data forthcoming.
Names: Intelligent Education
Title: BRIGHT NOTES: The Philosophy of St. Thomas Aquinas
Subject: STU004000 STUDY AIDS / Book Notes

CONTENTS

1)	Introduction to St. Thomas Aquinas	1
2)	Introduction to Summa Contra Gentiles	17
3)	Textual Analysis	19
	Book I	19
	Book II	23
	Book III	27
	Part I	52
	Part I-II	94
	Part II-III	121
4)	On Kingship	146
5)	Essay Questions and Answers	150
6)	Bibliography	158

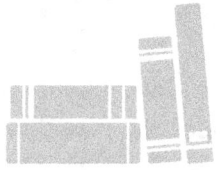

INTRODUCTION TO ST. THOMAS AQUINAS

Thomas Aquinas is not only one of the world's most influential philosophers, he also ranks among its leading theologians. In fact, he thought of himself primarily as a theologian; that is, he was mainly interested in interpreting life and reality in the light of divine revelation as found in the Bible and the teachings of his church. To do this well, he needed as a point of reference a philosophy, an understanding of the universe that was based only on reason and experience. Since he considered the available philosophies inadequate, he was forced to work out his own. He developed a world view that was so comprehensive and satisfying that it has never since lacked adherents. It is this philosophy, without the theological superstructure, that we shall take up in this book.

Aquinas gave us the most full and mature **exposition** of his philosophy in his two main theological works, the *Summa Theologica* and the *Summa Contra Gentiles*. (These are the original Latin names under which they continue to be known-they mean *Summa of Theology* and *Summa Against the Unbelievers*.) We shall base our presentation on these two titles and a short pamphlet entitled *De Regimine Principum*, which is usually translated *On the Government of Princes* or *On Kingship*, supplementing when necessary with references to his other books.

Our basic aims are (1) to explain Aquinas' main ideas, (2) to show their interrelations, (3) to relate them to their sources in other philosophies and (4) to comment on their relevance for us. Our ultimate hope is that we may, by helping the reader understand Thomas better, enable him to formulate for himself a more adequate philosophy of life.

EVOLUTION OF MEDIEVAL CULTURE

Aquinas is a typically medieval man. To understand him and how he came to develop his philosophy we must keep in mind some of the main events of the previous two thousand years. The civilization of antiquity reached its acme in the fifth and fourth centuries B.C. in Greece; its philosophic giants were Plato and Aristotle. Grecian culture then established itself throughout the Near East as a result of the conquests of Alexander. Meanwhile, Roman power was growing too, and by the beginning of the Christian era the Roman Empire included all of the civilized world of the West. As a result both Greek thought and the Christian religion could easily diffuse themselves. By A. D. 500, however, the western half of the Roman Empire had fallen to invading Germanic tribes, and Europe entered into the Dark Ages. In the succeeding centuries it was mainly the monasteries which maintained, however feebly, the remnants of learning. Only in the thirteenth century did Europe regain a cultural level equal to that of antiquity. The major civilizing influence was the Church, which dominated the hearts of men with her creed, cult and crusades, while gradually teaching them to appreciate the knowledge the monks had taken such pains to preserve.

THE UNIVERSITIES

In the first half of the Middle Ages education was a very primitive affair, conducted mostly in monastery and cathedral schools with a curriculum that we could describe as covering in an extremely watered-down fashion about half of what is nowadays studied in elementary and high school. The intellectual renaissance of the twelfth and thirteenth centuries was made possible by the founding at that time of numerous universities. They established new and advanced curricula (arts, canon and civil law, theology and medicine), and through exams and degrees sought to maintain high levels of academic achievement. By bringing together under challenging conditions large numbers of the best teachers and students of Europe, the universities became the center of intellectual life and advance. That of Paris was recognized as the greatest of them all. St. Thomas spent fifteen years there.

NEW TRANSLATIONS

A major factor stimulating progress at this same time was the translation into Latin of many previously unknown works of Aristotle and of Moslem and Jewish philosophers. It presented Europe with some completely new, different and rationally elaborated interpretations of the universe which demanded to be either accepted or refuted. The assimilation of these ideas resulted in a series of intellectual crises for Europe, many of whose effects are still with us, e.g., the various schools of scholastic philosophy and many of the differences between Catholics and Protestants.

MENDICANT ORDERS

An event important for Aquinas, and for the Middle Ages, was the founding of the Franciscans and the Dominicans at the beginning of the thirteenth century. They are called mendicant orders, because originally they supported themselves by begging. Their purpose was, like that of the monastery orders, to serve the Church, but unlike monks they moved about from one place to another and devoted themselves to active lives of preaching and teaching. To do this well, however, they had to provide their members with the best academic training possible. This was not too difficult, owing to their very fast growth in both numbers and means. But besides this they also encouraged and supported their more promising men to do research. As a result, the majority of influential thinkers from the thirteenth century to the Reformation belonged to one or the other of these orders. St. Albert and St. Thomas were Dominicans; St. Bonaventure, Roger Bacon, Scotus and Ockham were Franciscans.

MAIN PHILOSOPHIC INFLUENCES

Aristotle

The philosopher who influenced Aquinas the most was undoubtedly Aristotle. He was known in the earlier part of the Middle Ages only through portions of his logic. In the twelfth and thirteenth centuries almost all his works were translated into Latin. That Aquinas valued them most highly is clear insofar as he wrote detailed commentaries on most of them, that they might be better understood. From them he also received many of his basic concepts and theories. Among the latter we might mention first the notions of potentiality and actuality. Potentiality means the capacity to take on any perfection or determination. God is the only being who has no potentiality within him, who is pure actuality. All other beings are various combinations of actuality and potentiality. Thus all physical objects are made up of substance and accidents, the former being in potency (potentiality) to receive the latter. Accidents are such attributes as quality, quantity, relation and action which are found in a substance. Substance, on the other hand, does not exist in any further substrate (substance) but merely by itself. Thus it can serve as a foundation to receive the accidents. It is itself, however, composed of prime matter and substantial form. Prime matter is pure potency, the sheer capacity to take on various substantial forms. Substantial form consists of those determinant characteristics which make an object be the kind it is, for instance, a man or a horse. Aquinas also accepted most of Aristotle's theory of knowledge: the distinction between sense and intellectual knowledge, the passivity of the subject in relation to the object, the explanation of the origin of concepts through the theory of abstraction. Besides these, Aquinas also follows Aristotle more or less closely on many questions of ethics and in his view of knowledge as man's most valuable activity.

Augustine

In the Middle Ages St. Augustine was generally considered the supreme authority in theology and philosophy. Aquinas based much of his theology on Augustine's but was much more independent in regard to philosophical questions. Augustine held to a Christianized neoplatonism which Thomas thought was in urgent need of correction and completion through Aristotelian theories. In certain areas, however, Augustine's influence is clear: for instance, in the way in which Aquinas conceives of the attributes of God, divine knowledge, the relation of God to the universe, the nature and origin of evil, the immateriality of the human soul and the moral laws.

Moslem Philosophers

After its founding in the seventh century, Islam very quickly took over most of the Near East and northern Africa. While Europe was just beginning to work its way out of the Dark Ages, Moslem lands had a flourishing civilization. They eventually produced several notable philosophers, the greatest of whom were Avicenna and Averroes. These philosophers were basically Aristotelian, but they added neoplatonic overtones. Their works, many of which were commentaries on Aristotle, were translated into Latin at the same time as Aristotle's and thus helped to make him more widely known. Although often aided by the Moslem interpretation of Aristotle, Aquinas criticized it severely on some crucial points, such as the immortality of the soul and the unicity (oneness) of the intellect. Cardinal doctrines which he adopted from them include the real distinction of essence and existence in creatures and their identity in God.

Jewish Philosophers

Under the Moslems in Spain during the eleventh and twelfth centuries, the Jewish community prospered and produced two remarkable philosophers. Avencebrol, the author of The Source of Life, defended in it several views, such as the plurality of forms in an object, which were accepted by many Christian thinkers but rejected for the most part by Aquinas. On the other hand, Moses Maimonides, who wrote the classic Guide for the Perplexed, seems to have provided Thomas with an understanding of the proper relationship between reason and faith and with a solution to the question of whether the fact of creation in time can be proven philosophically. His answer: it cannot be proven, but it can be shown to be possible.

Neoplatonism

In the third century A.D., Plotinus, an Egyptian who opened a school of philosophy at Rome, combined divers ideas of Plato, Aristotle, the Stoics and himself into an original synthesis known as neoplatonism. This philosophy influenced Aquinas indirectly through Augustine and the Moslem and Jewish thinkers who had all accepted various neoplatonic views. It influenced him directly through such works as Dionysius' *On the Divine Names* and Proclus' *Book on Causes.* Thomas wrote commentaries on both these works and got some of his ideas concerning angels and causality from them.

The Stoics

Another group of philosophers who had a strong though indirect influence on Aquinas were the Stoics, who flourished from the third century B.C. to the third century A.D. They had worked out a detailed theory of the natural law. Conceiving of the universe as arranged according to a rational divine plan, they held that man could by his reason determine what acts were required or prohibited by nature to fulfill this divine plan. This idea of a natural moral law was taken up by Augustine, from whom it was accepted by everyone in the Middle Ages.

EARLY YEARS

Thomas Aquinas was born in 1225 near Aquino, halfway between Naples and Rome. His family was an old one, of the lower nobility. At the age of five he was sent to the abbey of Montecassino, apparently in the hope that he would eventually become abbot. There he received his elementary education under a Benedictine monk. Political turmoil and an impending war in the area caused him to leave at the age of twelve. About two years later he entered the University of Naples. He studied there about four years, becoming acquainted with both Aristotelian philosophy, just being introduced into the West, and the new Dominican Order, which he decided to join. The news of his action upset his mother, who hastened to Naples to talk him out of it. His superiors, however, had foreseen such a reaction and had already sent him on his way to Paris. His mother thereupon sent her other sons in pursuit. They brought him back, and he remained a prisoner in the family castles for two years. Since all attempts to make him change his mind had failed, he was then released. He went to Rome and then to Cologne, where he studied for several years under Albert the Great and was ordained.

Paris

In 1252 Thomas started graduate work at the University of Paris. He was at the same time giving courses on the Bible and on Peter the Lombard's *Sentences,* the standard theological text of that time. He introduced many innovations in his lectures, which also attracted notice for their lucidity and depth, and started to write. Among these early works are the pamphlet *On Being and Essence* and a lengthy *Commentary on the Sentences.*

Meanwhile the Dominicans and Franciscans were getting into hot water at the University. Their success in attracting students and in acquiring professorial chairs excited the ire of the secular clergy, who had had the teaching completely in their own hands before the recent arrival of the orders. Under the leadership of William of Saint-Amour the seculars started a concerted campaign of political maneuvering, libelous preaching and pamphleteering and even violence to get rid of their rivals. As a result of this dissension Thomas did not immediately receive full membership in the university Corporation of Masters when he completed his requirements. However, the whole affair was straightened out at the end of 1256 through papal intervention. His position of Master of Theology being recognized, he remained in Paris for three more years, teaching and writing On Truth and the first book of the *Summa Contra Gentiles*.

Italy

In 1259 he returned to his homeland. During the next ten years he traveled to various cities in fulfillment of duties in connection with his order or the papal court. He continued to teach and preach but had much more free time. Thus he was able to finish the *Summa Contra Gentiles* and to start the *Summa Theologica*, besides composing a number of shorter books. Among the latter were commentaries on several works of Aristotle. These are important because the translations of Aristotle available up to then were often defective. To remedy this, Thomas had requested a fellow Dominican, William of Moerbeke, who was an accomplished Greek scholar, to make new ones. With these Thomas was able to arrive at a much better understanding of Aristotle, and he preserved these new insights in his commentaries.

Paris Again

In 1269 Aquinas returned to the University of Paris, which was again in a turmoil. The followers of William of Saint-Amour had renewed their attacks on the friars. Thomas, working with the Franciscan Bonaventure, again refuted them in pamphlets and university sermons and eventually gained the day. At the same time trouble of another sort was brewing. Many professors, including numerous Franciscans, objected to the introduction of many of the Aristotelian doctrines which Aquinas was championing. The result was a series of debates, which he usually won, but also the condemnation later on of several of his views by the bishop of Paris. Meanwhile Thomas was also busy on a third front. A new philosophical movement known as "Averroism," because it followed Averroes' pantheistic and neoplatonic interpretation of Aristotle, was spreading in the university. Thomas combated it in the classroom, in the chapel and in writing. He was able to check it growth for the time being, but the movement maintained itself till the end of the Middle Ages. Besides this he was also writing some more commentaries on the Bible and Aristotle and working on the *Summa Theologica*.

Last Years

In 1272 Thomas was recalled to Italy and a given a free hand in setting up a new theological seminary for the Dominicans. For its site he chose Naples and started to lecture that autumn. In 1274 he started off for Lyons, having been summoned by the pope to attend the council to be held there. He took sick on the way and died on March 7. Forty-nine years later he was canonized.

NATURE OF AQUINAS' PHILOSOPHY

Characteristic Doctrines

In Thomas' view, since all truth has a single source, God, a true philosophy and a true theology will never contradict each other. Hence a combination of faith and reason constitutes the highest life. The central, unifying idea of his philosophy in his notion of being or existence as the supreme actuality. God is simply sheer existence without any limitation and makes all things to be by merely willing their participation in his being. He is also therefore absolutely simple, perfect, good, omnipotent, immutable and one. Although all creatures exist only insofar as they participate in God's being, they do not all participate in God's being, they do not all participate in it to the same degree, hence the different types of beings we find in the universe. As a further result, different objects also have a different **metaphysical** structure; that is, they are made to be precisely what they are by the interrelations and variations of their ultimate constitutive factors. Technically these are known as prime matter and substantial form, substance and accidents, quiddity (or essence) and existence. Each of these sets represents a relationship of potentiality to actuality. There are three main types of creatures. Spirits are those whose being is so little restricted by the limitations resulting from potentiality that they are not subject to substantial changes or the dimensions of time and space. Material beings on the other hand are so restricted. Men belong to the material world, but their souls are such that they can transcend it; that is, men are both material and spiritual. Men have as properties of their souls various capacities or powers of action. Among them are the senses, by which we know material objects in a limited, material way; the intellect, by which we can know any being in a superior, immaterial manner;

the sense appetites, by which we tend to sensed, physical goods; and the will, by which we can through free choice desire any known good. The senses and intellect enable us to know things only incompletely but objectively; that is, as they really are. The dignity of man results from his capacity of knowing and choosing between all the goods available to him. But he demeans himself if he does not choose the end for which God made him: an ultimate union through knowledge and love with God himself. The purpose of this life therefore is to perfect our natures through the practice of the virtues and the avoidance of all vices, that we might achieve both now and in the future life the fullest possible relationship between our and the divine personalities.

His Originality

In the eyes of his contemporaries Thomas was not merely an innovator but a revolutionary. In the eight centuries preceding, Augustinian thought had dominated Western thought. It continued indeed to exert a tremendous influence all through the Middle Ages. Thomas, however, rejected this dominance and sought to install in its place a synthesis with a more Aristotelian basis. To many of his contemporaries this seemed so radical as to be heretical, and the result was the ecclesiastical condemnation in 1277 of certain Thomistic doctrines.

From a wider historical perspective Thomas' originality takes on a different look. He is seen as one of the greatest synthesizers of all times. He did not value novelty for its own sake. Rather, he felt the main task to be to point out and preserve whatever truths previous thinkers had discovered. This did not prevent him from working out new answers of his own to certain problems, but it does mean that he deliberately set out to build his system with ideas and doctrines that earlier thinkers had developed. What makes his achievement remarkable is that in using the philosophic views of various men he subtly and often radically changed their meaning to make them conform to his own insights into the nature of reality. These views, which in their original form were incompatible or even contradictory, he transformed and wove into a unified, dynamic and comprehensive explanation of the whole universe.

The central notion of his philosophy, and one that is completely original with him, is that of the primacy of existence. The vast majority of philosophers have been essentialists; that is, in their interpretation of reality they hold that to be real is to have an essence, is to be a certain kind of thing; existence is considered to be only a more or less unimportant aspect of essence. Thomas, however, is an "existentialist." He maintains that existence is what makes an essence real, that essence is merely a limitation of existence and that therefore existence is the most basic and important factor in the **metaphysical** constitution of any object. Note, however, that Thomas is not an existentialist in the sense that contemporary thinkers like Sartre and Heidegger are. These men are called existentialists only because they base their speculations on what they call the existential aspects of reality: the personal experience we have of the emptiness or irrationality of life is conquered or transcended by our free choices.

WORKS

Summas

The summa was a common literary form in the Middle Ages. It was a detailed, systematic study of a given problem or area. Thomas wrote two of them. The *Summa Theologica* is his masterpiece and was written as an introductory text for the study of theology. It is a multivolume work, but its organization is so logical and simple that it is relatively easy to find one's way around in it. It is divided into three main parts. Part I deals with God and his creatures. Part II is concerned with how man should act and it is itself divided into two sub-parts. Part III treats of Christ and his work. Each part is broken down into "questions." The shortest part has ninety; the longest, one hundred and eighty-nine questions. Each question consists of about a half-dozen articles. Every article has the same set form: a statement of the problem, a list of objections against the author's view, the general solution proposed by the author and his responses to each of the objections.

Comment

His use of this set form makes it possible to find whatever you want very quickly. It also enables you to skip large portions of the text - the objections and the responses - without missing the main points, which are given in the general solution. The latter is always preceded by the words "I answer that."

The *Summa Contra Gentiles* is a textbook of philosophy and theology written for the use of young Dominicans. It is divided into four books. Each deals respectively with God, creatures, morality and dogma. Thomas did not write it in the question and article form but simply divided each book into chapters.

Commentaries

University education in the Middle Ages consisted to a large extent of the study of the recognized classics. Very often a course consisted of a line-by-line explanation by the professor of one of them. The written version of such a course or any work similar to it constitutes the **genre** of the commentary. St. Thomas wrote many of them. One of his earliest and longest works is his commentary on Peter the Lombard's *Sentences,* which was the standard theological text of the time. It is of importance for us today inasmuch as it enables us to determine on what points he later changed his mind. The commentary on Boethius' *On the Trinity* is valuable because it contains a long **exposition** of Thomas' notion of science. It also explains his views on neoplatonism, as do too his commentaries of *On the Weeks* by Boethius, *On the Divine Names* by Dionysius and *On Causes* by Proclus. Philosophically the most important commentaries are those on Aristotle, all of which were not finished. They cover Aristotle's main philosophical works: *The Organon, Physics, Metaphysics, Ethics, Politics, On the Soul* and several lesser books. The scriptural commentaries are only of theological interest.

Questions

The question was another characteristic medieval form. It was of two types, the disputed and the quodlibetal. They also resulted from the way university teaching was carried on. Teachers and students regularly met for "disputations," in which a given topic was debated. The question was the write-up in which the teacher afterwards summarized the debate. In a disputed question the topic was chosen before time by the teacher; in the quodlibetal question it was proposed by the audience. Thomas wrote a number of questions of both types. Especially important are those on truth, potency, evil, the soul and the virtues.

Shorter Works

Thomas wrote about three dozen of these. Among the more notable are *On Being and Essence,* which is perhaps his first work and the one in which we find sketched his theory of the primacy of existence; *On the Unity of the Intellect*, in which he refuted the Averroists; and *On Kingship*. Another noteworthy item, because it is so different, is the office for the feast of Corpus Christi, which contains some of the most magnificent poetry of the Middle Ages.

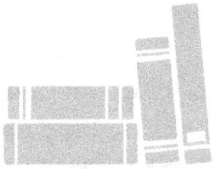

INTRODUCTION TO SUMMA CONTRA GENTILES

ITS PURPOSE AND COMPOSITION

The title of this work means "a summa against the unbelievers." According to one old story, St. Thomas was supposed to have been asked to write it by a Spanish Dominican for use in training missionaries to the Moslems. It seems more likely, however, that he intended it for a much wider audience and purpose, as a textbook for all Dominicans and others who were starting their university studies. It resembles modern works more than does the *Summa Theologica* because it avoids the medieval format of questions and articles. It consists of four books, each containing about a hundred relatively short chapters. It does not in general present detailed discussions, but rather only his conclusions with the briefest possible statement of his reasons for them.

COMPARISON WITH THE SUMMA THEOLOGICA

The *Summa Contra Gentiles* was finished just before the *Summa Theoligica* was begun. Although they are both theological works, the former is more thoroughly philosophical since the first three books take up the truths which serve as a basis for the study of theology but which are demonstrable by man's unaided reason, such as the existence and nature of God, the nature of man and what is proper human behavior. Only in the fourth book are the dogmas of revelation discussed. Both the general structure and the articulation of the parts are simpler in the *Summa Contra Gentiles*. As a result, however, it is also much less full and rich in the variety of problems treated and of solutions proposed. It has many fewer references to other thinkers. It takes up the major problems but only outlines Thomas' answers to them. In other words, it seems to represent a preliminary version of the *Summa Theologica*. Nevertheless, it discusses some points more thoroughly than the *Summa Theologica* does. These are the ones that we shall discuss here, leaving the others till we meet them in the *Summa Theologica*.

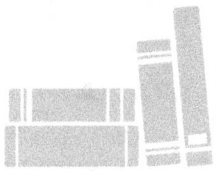

SUMMA CONTRA GENTILES

TEXTUAL ANALYSIS

BOOK I

WISDOM

To be wise means to be able to order things rightly and to govern them well. It entails then that one always keep in mind the end to be achieved. The ultimate end of all things, however, is that which is intended by the first cause. But the first cause, as we shall show, is an intellect. Since the good of an intellect is truth, the ultimate end of the whole universe is truth. Thus the contemplation of truth is the main characteristic of the wise man. As a result, we call the science of the truth which is the source of all other truth, first philosophy, metaphysics or wisdom. Its two main tasks then are to uncover the truth and to denounce errors. It follows also that the quest for wisdom is the most perfect, sublime, useful and sweet of all. Book I inquires into the existence and nature of this first truth, which we call God.

TYPES AND SOURCES OF TRUTH

When it is a question of knowing about God, there are two kinds of true propositions that we can attain. Some truths, like the existence of God, can be known by us merely through the normal use of our cognitive powers. Others, like the Trinity, exceed the reach of our unaided powers. The latter then can be known only through divine revelation. The former, however, may also be revealed to us by God and often are, since otherwise many men would never know them with certitude because they lack the necessary intelligence, training or occasion. Then too, without revelation it would take us a long time to discover these truths, and even then many doubts and errors would remain. However, some thinkers have maintained that we should never accept as true anything which we cannot prove to be such by reason only. Such a view is unwarranted though, because it uselessly prevents us from accepting truths of the greatest value. Note too that what we accept on faith in the Christian religion is not without corroboration. On the contrary, its truth is supported by numerous and continuing miracles. Moreover, there is no possibility that these two kinds of truth will ever contradict each other, since they both come ultimately from the same source.

HOW WE KNOW GOD

After outlining five ways of proving God's existence, Aquinas pointed out that in seeking to understand what God is, we must use for the most part the way of remotion or negation. For, God as he is in himself is beyond our understanding. But we can form a more or less adequate notion of him by knowing what he is not. The more predicates we know we can deny of him, that much closer are we to a realization of what he is like. Thus, by denying that God is an accident and a body, we distinguish him from them and so to that extent came closer to what he is. Such a negative kind of knowledge is obviously very imperfect since it involves only an awareness of what he is not.

THE NATURE OF GOD

In the demonstration of God's existence it was established that he does not change. From this it follows then that he is eternal (has no beginning or end), that there is no potentiality in him, that he is not material, for all material things can change, and that there is in him no composition of parts of any sort. From this Aquinas concludes further that God is in his own essence, quiddity or nature. This is something we can say only of him, because creatures are not said to be their quiddity, but only to have one. This is because they are composed of existence and quiddity. Such a composite only has a quiddity. But since there is no composition in God he does not have a quiddity. Rather, his quiddity and he are simply and absolutely identical. Carrying this a step further, we must also say that in God quiddity and existence are identical too. Aquinas gives a number of arguments to prove this, besides the one from the lack of composition in God. One of them he formulated in this manner. Existence denominates a certain act or perfection. But whenever there is in a being an act and something distinct from that act, the latter is in potency to the former. There is, however, no potency in God, as was seen in the proofs for his existence. Hence, in him quiddity and existence are the same.

Comment

To understand what Aquinas means here, we must know the meaning of the technical terms he uses. The finite, limited beings that we experience are all composites, that is, they are ultimately constituted of several factors or principles. These cannot exist independently of the composite or of each other. Among these principles are existence and quiddity. Existence is the factor that makes the composite be. Quiddity is the factor that makes the composite be precisely what it is, that makes it have every other determinate characteristic that it has. Thus quiddity is in potency in relation to existence, and existence actualizes the quiddity, makes it actually be. What Aquinas is saying is that in God there is no such composition. Existence and quiddity, which in finite beings are really distinct factors and which by their union constitute those beings, in God are only logically distinct, are really identical. In other words, God's quiddity, what makes him be divine, is simply to exist.

In the rest of Book I Aquinas discusses at some length various attributes and operations of God, such as his intellect and will. These topics are treated more fully, however, in the *Summa Theologica*.

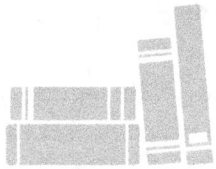

SUMMA CONTRA GENTILES

TEXTUAL ANALYSIS

BOOK II

....

PURPOSE

In this book Aquinas first takes up God considered as creator of the universe; then, what he created, with most of the attention going to the nature of man. Unlike the *Summa Theologica*, which discusses the angels at length, this work has little to say about them. Most of the questions which Aquinas treated of in this book he later took up again in the *Summa Theologica*.

MULTIPLICITY OF OBJECTS

One point which the *Summa Contra Gentiles* discusses at length (ch. 39 ff.) is the variety of beings found in the universe. This cannot result from chance, nor from mere potentiality to variety, nor because of the diversity of causes. It is caused rather by one most perfect agent, God. Like all causes, God seeks to bring about in his effects as full a manifestation of his creative power as is possible in such effects. He cannot, however, be adequately reflected through just one type of creature. In order therefore to manifest as perfectly as possible his goodness, he must create both a variety and multiplicity of objects. They run the whole range from inert, lifeless minerals to angels.

INTELLECTUAL SUBSTANCES

The most perfect of these creatures are the substances which, having an intellect, also possess will and freedom. Such intellectual substances are the opposite of physical substances or bodies. Purely physical substances can know only other bodies. But since intellectual substances can know many other things besides bodies they are not themselves bodies but the contrary kind of substance. This is why they are called spirits. Another reason why we know that spirits are the contrary kind of substance to bodies is that bodies, being physical, can affect themselves only by one part acting on another. The intellect, however, can reflect back on itself. The whole intellect can know the whole of itself. Thus intellectual substances are not physical; that is, they are immaterial. To put it in another way, physical substances are extended, have parts outside of parts and are perceivable by the senses. Spirits have no extension, do not have quantitative parts and are not sensibly perceivable.

Metaphysical Structure

This variety of creatures indicates that their basic, metaphysical structure, the combination of factors which constitute them, is different. These factors or principles are forms either of act (actuality) or potency (potentiality). Act is any perfection or determination. Potency is the capacity to take on an act. For instance, an infant is, in act, only an infant; in potency it is an adult. Now, in creatures, that which makes them be the kind of thing they are and that which makes them be are two distinct principles. The former we call substance; and the latter, existence. Substance and existence are factors that are really distinct from each other because the substance as it is being generated is in potency to exist, and potency is distinct from its act. Then too, in the creature there is only an incidental unity of substance and existence, which obviously could not be if they were identical. In physical beings, however, there is also, besides the composition of substance and existence, that of prime matter and substantial form. Prime matter is completely indeterminate potentiality. It is simply the capacity to be any kind of physical substance. Substantial form is the act or perfection which determines prime matter and which with it constitutes a substance. Form and matter are thus another act-potency set.

Comment

Besides the twofold composition mentioned here, Aquinas also admits, following Aristotle, a third between the substance and its accidents. The accidents are of nine sorts: quantity, quality, relation, action, passion, when, where, position and condition. They are all acts in relation to substance, which is in potency to them. Thus, in physical beings the **metaphysical** structure consists of the following principles: prime matter is actualized by substantial form and the composite of the two forms substance; substance is actualized by the accidents and the resulting composite forms the quiddity; quiddity is actualized by existence and the composite thereby formed is the individual object, such as this horse or this man. The bond between each of these sets of principles is the act-potency relationship. The act determines the potency, makes it actually such and such. The potency limits the act; it allows only so much of the actuality to come through and no more.

We should be careful not to confuse prime matter with matter in the usual sense of the word. Colloquially, matter means anything which is perceptible by the senses, such as a table. Prime matter on the other hand is not perceivable by the senses, but is only known through inference by the intellect. Nor is it even a being. It is only a principle of being. It makes real things possible by acting as a substratum for the various determinations which it receives. So, for a physical being like man we have a prime matter receiving the substantial form of "humanity," as a result of which is a composite that is characterized as both animal and rational. This substance is further determined by the accidents: for instance, two hundred pounds, white, American, working, etc. The ultimate actualization of really being is conferred to all of this by existence. In angels there is only a composition of substance-accidents and quiddity-existence. While in God there is no composition whatever, quiddity and existence in him being simply identical.

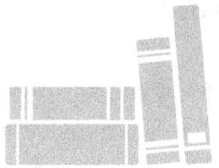

SUMMA CONTRA GENTILES

TEXTUAL ANALYSIS

BOOK III

PURPOSE

After having discussed the existence and nature of God and how he is the creator of a vast variety of beings, in this book Aquinas explains how God is also the end and ruler of all things, but whose mode of governing varies depending on whether the beings involved are rational or not.

ALL ACTIVITY TELEOLOGICAL

Every agent is tending in his activity to some end. It does not make any difference whether the agent is capable of knowledge or not. Thus, both the archer in shooting and the arrow in its flight have an end: to hit the bull's eye. Note too that the end sought is always a determinate one. No action is ever done without a particular goal being aimed at. Sometimes this goal is some object to be produced, as when a contractor builds a house. Sometimes, however, the action is done for its own sake, as in the satisfaction of one's curiosity. That goal beyond which no further one is sought is called the ultimate end. Every action is also done for an ultimate end, because if it were not, the agent would be tending to an infinity of ends. But this is impossible: since the infinite cannot be traversed, the agent would never start to act for such an impossible goal. Then too, if an agent did not aim at some particular goal, it would be indifferent to all of them and would never act. There are some actions, however, that might seem to have no end; for instance, play, contemplation or those, like scratching, done without thinking. These really all have an end though. Contemplation is its own end. Play sometimes is too, but at other times it may be for the purpose of preparing oneself to do something else. Scratching and similar acts, even when done unconsciously, serve to relieve physical tension.

ALL ACTIVITY FOR A GOOD

The end which every agent seeks is a good for it. For by good is meant whatever satisfies a need. Then, too, every action and change tend to bring about a new perfection or actuality. If the action is its own end, then it is the agent himself who is perfected. If the action terminates in something outside of the agent, then its purpose is to perfect it. Perfection and goodness are, however, synonymous. So every end is a good. And so is it, too, that philosophers define the good as that which all things tend to. From this it follows that whatever evil effects are brought about by an action are not wanted as such by the agent. Evil effects occur incidentally in the quest of some good, as a result sometimes of some defect in the agent. This is not to deny that these evil effects are often foreseen and willed indirectly, for this happens frequently. Thus when a man commits adultery he does not do it primarily to achieve the evil effect of breaking the moral law. Rather, he desires the physical pleasure which is a good and which is his main end. The moral evil involved is accepted as part of achieving the physical good.

GOD IS THE END OF ALL THINGS

As we have seen, every activity is ordered to some good as its ultimate end. However, since an end is such only insofar as it is a good, it is only the good as such that can be an end. Thus the highest good would have to also be the highest end. But there is only one supreme good, which is God. Therefore every activity is ordered to a unique good, which is God, as its ultimate end. Then, too, insofar as the most perfect being in every genus is the cause of all others within that genus, God as the supreme good is the cause of the goodness of every lesser good. He is therefore also the cause of every end being an end. But he is then the supreme end of all things. Moreover, in every series of related ends the ultimate end of the series is the reason why every other end is a part of the series. But everything in the world has a certain degree of goodness. As a result, since finality is founded on goodness, every lesser good which is an end is ordered to God as its ultimate end. Thus we must again conclude that God is the ultimate end of all.

HOW CREATURES TEND TO GOD

To the extent that they share in the divine goodness, creatures become similar to God. For them to tend to God as their ultimate end means, therefore, to participate more and more in his goodness and thus become ever more similar to him. In this sense we can say that the end of all creatures is to be assimilated to God. However, although they seek in their own way to copy the divine goodness, none of them participates in it to the extent of possessing it in the same manner that God does. They are assimilated to God by simply existing, by tending to the perfection proper to their species and by becoming causes. Thus, even objects incapable of knowledge tend toward God, inasmuch as they achieve a good when they are directed to some end by an intelligent agent or by the natural inclinations placed in them by God.

MAN'S END

God is the end of man, as he is the end of all things. Intellectual creatures, however, tend to him in a special manner, by knowing him. This is to be expected because every being tends to his end in the way in which he can most perfectly achieve it. For intellectual substances this clearly will be through cognition of God. We could also argue in this way. One of the ends of every being is the performance of the operation proper to it, since it is thereby perfected. To understand, however, is the characteristic operation of intellectual substances and is therefore also their end. But the most perfect form of this operation would be their ultimate end. The higher the object known, however, the more perfect is the act of understanding. Thus, to understand the most perfect intelligible, which is God, is the most perfect act of this sort. Thus the intellectual knowledge of God is the ultimate end of every man.

THE ROLE OF THE WILL

Since man can attain to God not only through his intellect but also through his will, by desiring, loving and rejoicing in him, it might seem that man's ultimate end and happiness would consist in the love of God, or some other act of the will. Various arguments could be proposed in support of this. (1) What constitutes anything as an end is its goodness, which is the object of the will; that is, goodness is what the will is structured to react to primarily. But the object of the intellect is truth, which cannot be an end except insofar as it is a good. Thus man's ultimate end must be achieved through an act of the will. (2) Pleasure is the ultimate perfection of any operation and it also is an act of the will. But if man's ultimate end is the perfection of his operation, then this end would have to rest in the will. (3) Moreover, pleasure seems to be desired for itself more than anything else. But to be sought for itself is characteristic of the ultimate end. (4) Then, too, all agree that they seek the ultimate end. But more people seek pleasure than knowledge. Hence pleasure must be our end. (5) It seems also that the will is a higher power than the intellect, since it moves the intellect to act. Thus our ultimate end would have to consist in an act of the will. St. Thomas avers, however, that none of these arguments is correct. For as happiness is the proper good of intellectual substances, it can be achieved only through what is characteristic of such a nature, namely the intellect. An appetite, however, which is what the will is, is not characteristic of an intellectual nature since it is found in brutes and even in things incapable of knowledge. Then, too, the object of any power is prior by nature to any action of that power. So, happiness, as the ultimate end of the will, cannot be identical with any of its actions.

We should note further that whatever perfects an object is not necessarily its end. Thus pleasure, since it is only an accidental and not a substantial perfection of the agent, is not itself an end. On the contrary, it is ordered to the good of the agent and his activity. Activities are accompanied by pleasures to ensure that they will be performed. As a result, pleasures, instead of being our ultimate end, are on the contrary capable of being either good or bad, depending on the operation they result from. If they follow on a morally desirable operation they are good; they are bad if they accompany an evil action. Then, too, the fact that pleasures are not sought for some further goal does not make them our ultimate end. The reason for this is that pleasure is simply a concomitant to the achievement of any end. Nor is it true that more people seek pleasure than seek knowledge, although it could be admitted that more people are interested in sense knowledge and the pleasures thereof than are concerned with intellectual knowledge and pleasures. But this is because all our knowledge begins on the sense level. It is also false that the will is a higher power than the intellect, for the will causes the intellect to act only incidentally. Because the act of understanding is a good it is desired as such by the will, and this causes the intellect in fact to know. But the act of the will is caused in the first place by the intellect, by whose knowledge of the good the will is moved. Then too, the will puts the intellect in operation through a sort of efficient causality. The intellect, however, moves the will in the manner of a telic or final cause. But an efficient cause is posterior and lower. Hence it is clear that the intellect is in an absolute sense a higher power than the will, even though the latter may be superior from a given, limited point of view.

ERRORS CONCERNING HAPPINESS

It follows then that our happiness cannot consist primarily of physical pleasures, because the sense appetites are lower forms of faculties than the will. If the will and its pleasures cannot be man's end, much less could those of sense. Nor can honors make us happy, because honors are given to us by others, and happiness must result from inner perfection.

Likewise, riches cannot be man's supreme good, because wealth is not wanted for itself but only for what we can get with it. Similarly power, which is so unstable and so much a matter of chance, could not be the highest good. The same goes for such physical goods as health, beauty and strength. For these are possessed by both good and evil men, nor are they matters of choice. We could not say either that our ultimate happiness will consist of virtuous activity. The virtues are simply means to help us achieve certain ends; they are not the ends themselves. It is clear, too, that happiness cannot consist in artistic productivity. The purpose of the latter is to provide men with objects they can use for a better life, so it cannot itself be our end.

NATURE OF MAN'S ULTIMATE HAPPINESS

If happiness cannot consist ultimately of any of the above, we must conclude that it will be found only in the contemplation of truth. This is the only activity that is proper to man in the sense that the other animals do not share in it. Nor is it sought for anything except itself. Through it, too, we are assimilated to superior beings, since this is the one activity that we have in common with God and the angels. It is also the activity in which we are the most self-sufficient, requiring for it the minimum of exterior support. It is also to it that all our other actions seem ordered. For good health, the various necessities of life, the serenity of mind achieved through the moral virtues and prudence, the peace and order provided by civil society, all these and others, when rightly understood, are seen to have as their purpose making it possible and easier to contemplate truth. To be completely satisfying, however, our knowledge cannot be merely of general principles nor could it be a detailed understanding of the lower levels of reality. Rather, it must consist of wisdom, knowledge of all things, including God himself. However, the kind of knowledge of God required is not the usual confused type found in most men. As a result of seeing the order in the world they realize that there has to be some supreme being responsible for it, but they make all sorts of errors about who God is and what kind of being he is. But besides this way of knowing God there is also the scientific, demonstrated understanding of him, such as was developed in the previous book. Although this is by far superior, it does not tell us what God is so much as what he is not and how he is different from other beings. Hence it, too, would not suffice for perfect happiness.

Now we can also know God through faith in what he has revealed. Such knowledge is superior to the demonstrated in one way, insofar as by it we can know things about God which we otherwise would never even suspect. Considered simply as a mode of cognition, however, it is most imperfect, since in it the intellect does not grasp in itself that to which it assents. Thus it could not provide perfect happiness either. But we have yet another, more positive way of knowing God, through the similarity between him and our own spiritual nature. But this form of analogical cognition is also rather vague and imperfect. Thus, since every way that we have in this life of knowing God is insufficient to give us perfect happiness, this, we must conclude, cannot be achieved in this life, only in the next. That conclusion follows also from the fact that perfect happiness would include the fulfillment of all natural appetites, so that nothing further would be desired. But this obviously never occurs in this life. Only in the next life, then, will the natural desire, which cannot be futile, to possess the divine truth be fulfilled through a direct intellectual vision of the divine essence. This clearly can be the effect only of a special divine aid.

DIVINE GOVERNMENT

After discussing how God is the end of all things, Aquinas then takes up the question of whether and how he governs the world. That he rules the world is clear from the fact that he made it and is its end. For whoever makes something for a given end always arranges its various parts so that they will tend to that end. And that is what it is to govern. But since God rules the world, from this it also follows that he conserves it in existence, for governing involves taking care of everything necessary to achieve an end. But God's end, which is to manifest his goodness, is achieved not only through the activities of his creatures, but also through their very existence. Then too, since to conserve a thing is simply to maintain it in existence, the cause of a thing's existence is also what conserves it. And we have seen that God is the cause of the being of all things.

GOD HELPS TO PRODUCE EVERY BEING

This, it may be objected, contradicts experience. Do not parents alone generate children? No, says Aquinas, they have the concurrence of God. In the proofs of his existence, God is seen to be the first, uncaused cause and the end of every being and agent. But whenever a number of agents act together in a unified way under a single agent, the effects which they produce in common are produced by the individual agents only insofar as they are under the influence of the activity and power of the prime agent. Thus when an army wins a victory, it is caused primarily by the general, insofar as he was the one who directed each unit. So, since the common effect of all agents is to cause existence, they necessarily do this insofar as they are acting under God's influence and through his power.

We could also argue in this way. Whatever is by its very essence of a certain sort, is the proper cause of whatever is of the same sort in a limited, participated way. But only God is by his very nature existence, while everything else has existence through participation. Hence, the existence of every other being is the proper effect of God, so that whatever makes another to be does so only inasmuch as it acts as a funnel for the divine power.

GOD HELPS TO PRODUCE ALL ACTIVITY

From the preceding it follows that God also concurs in the activities of all his creatures. For, every agent causes something to be, either substantially or accidentally. But, as we have seen, nothing causes another to be except when God works through it. There have, however, been some philosophers, for instance among the Moslems, who have fallen into error of a contrary type, believing that creatures could not themselves cause anything but that God was the sole cause of every activity. According to these men creatures were completely passive, and whatever happens to them is the direct result of a renewed creation on the part of God. Thus they would say that is not the fire that warms us, but God, when we are in the presence of the fire. The reason they held to this is that they thought that any change consisted of bringing something out of nothing, which is creation; but since only God can create, then only he can cause. Thomas rejects this theory for a number of different reasons. One of them is that if this view were correct, then, since God's activity cannot be made different by things, all his effects would be the same. But experience clearly shows this not to be the case. Another argument is that it would be contrary to the divine wisdom to involve things in the production of effects if they had no positive role to play. Thus Thomas avers that things can be real causes, even though to be such requires the concurrence of God.

Comment

Were Aquinas alive today he would undoubtedly raise similar objections against contemporary phenomenalists who, following David Hume (1711-1776), also deny that causality in the traditional sense, of one thing making another come about, occurs. For them one event simply comes after another, without being brought about by the latter, and causality is merely the expectation we have that certain events will occur as they always have in the past. Aquinas would say that the phenomenalists are less reasonable than the Moslems, who at least admitted that there was a cause involved in every change.

HOW CONCURRENCE OCCURS

Certain difficulties can be raised against the view that God and creatures are both causes of the effects we see them producing. In the first place, it seems impossible that one action should be produced by two agents, so that if a creature brings about some effect it cannot be caused by God too. Secondly, it is unnecessary to postulate a number of causes for what can be adequately explained by only one, for nature always acts as economically as possible. Now since the divine power would suffice to produce any event, any finite causes are superfluous; alternatively, if a creature produces an effect, he should need no divine concurrence. To resolve such difficulties we must distinguish in every action the agent and the power by which it acts. The power of any inferior agent depends, however, on that of the superior agents that either give it to, or conserve it in, or apply it through, the inferior. Thus the activity of any inferior agent results not only from its own power but also from that of all its superiors, and they all simultaneously produce the one effect. They are then all causes, but each acts in its own way. And none of them is superfluous. God is not, because it is ultimately through his power that anything is produced. Finite causes are not either, because by producing effects they are thereby more similar to him.

COMPATIBILITY OF DIVINE PROVIDENCE AND HUMAN FREEDOM

It might also seem that God's foreknowledge and concurrence cannot be reconciled with the fact that man is free. A closer consideration, however, shows the opposite. Every ruler is more concerned with achieving and increasing what is more perfect than what is less perfect. However, the contingency found in irrational creatures results from their imperfection. For their nature determines them to a given course of action which they always follow, unless they are prevented through their own weakness, by some exterior cause or because of the unsuitability of the materials used. As a result they usually bring about the same effects in the same way, although they occasionally fail. On the other hand, the contingency of willed acts results from the perfection of the will. It is not restricted to one line of action but is able to produce a variety of effects. Divine providence will then be more concerned with preserving the liberty of the will than the contingency of natural causes. Moreover, it is characteristic of divine wisdom to use things in accordance with their natural modes of action. As, then, God has made humans free and inferior creatures determined by their natural appetites, he will necessarily preserve their natural mode of action when he cooperates with them to produce an effect.

PROVIDENCE, LUCK AND CHANCE

That there is a divine providence does not mean that there are no such things as luck and chance. For these refer to those events that occur infrequently. They result precisely because of the order established by God. For the greater perfection of the universe he has made it with all sorts of beings, including corruptible, defectible ones, which act upon one another. When two or more of them, in seeking their own ends, happen to cross each other's path and as a result either help or inhibit each other, it is unexpected, and so we say it happened by chance or luck. Thus if two men go to the store for food and meet each other, so that the one collects a debt from the other, that is his good luck. It is necessary that there be such chance events which occur occasionally. Otherwise everything would be necessary, and such a lack of contingent beings would be an imperfection for the universe and contrary to divine wisdom.

THE EXTENT OF PROVIDENCE

God's rule extends to every single being and action. This might seem to be untrue because of their contingency and because so much in them is a result of chance. As we have seen, however, neither contingency nor even freedom is incompatible with divine providence. If providence did not extend to every single thing, there could be several reasons for it: God does not know them, or he cannot extend his power that far, or he does not want to. However, God knows every being since he is the cause of them all. Being infinite, his power extends to all things and he loves every good. We must then conclude that his providence extends to even the slightest action.

FATE

Some people have denied both fate and providence because they consider only the immediate causes of things and they see so many of them happening by chance. Others, however, have sought to explain such events in terms of more ultimate causes. But some of these claim that the stars, or some similar finite cause, determine all events and they call such necessity fate. Our previous considerations clearly show them to be wrong. Others, however, have referred to divine providence as fate. As such a usage of terms is misleading, it is usually avoided.

CAN PROVIDENCE BE CERTAIN?

It might seem either that providence is not certain or that everything has to happen the way it does. In the first place, events occur either necessarily or contingently. If they occur contingently, then whatever providence intends, they need not occur. And so providence involves no certitude. In the second place, if providence is certain, then this inference must be true: "If God foresees something, it will happen." But God, being eternal, knows everything even before it happens, so everything that occurs is necessary. To see the fallacy in these arguments, says Thomas, we must remember that God as ruler of the universe wills everything that happens, to happen in the way that it does: either necessarily or contingently. To produce such effects he uses in the first case necessary causes and in the second, contingent ones. Thus, he not only produces all effects, but he makes some to be necessarily and others contingently. And so we speak of them as either necessary or contingent. In regard to that first argument, then, we can see that contingent events are known by God with certitude and from all eternity as contingent. In regard to the second argument, it is true that whatever God foresees will happen, but it will infallibly occur in the manner that he foresaw that it would, as necessary or contingent.

ARE PRAYERS OF ANY USE?

Just as providence does not impose necessity on what is foreseen, neither does it exclude the utility of prayer. This does not mean that prayers can change the eternal dispositions of providence. That would be impossible. But God, in his supreme goodness, takes into consideration from all eternity the prayers he knows will be offered to him and establishes the providential order accordingly. For it is of the nature of friendship to want to fulfill the desires of the loved one, as long as what he wants is for his own good and perfection. Thus is it that God often does not answer our prayers by granting what we ask, but rather by denying it or by giving us something else, because we ask for what is really not good for us. Our prayers then sometimes do cause certain effects to be produced. They are just like any of the other secondary causes God uses to bring about a more perfect order in the universe, one which approximates more closely to the divine goodness. To say that one should not pray to God in order to get something, because his providence is immutable, is as absurd as to say that we should not walk to arrive at a destination.

THE POSSIBILITY OF MIRACLES

As we have seen, the order established by God in the universe is achieved by a concatenation of causes. There is no reason, however, why he cannot produce effects in it by his direct activity, without making use of any subordinate causes. This is because of the difference between natural and voluntary causes. The former act only as they are made to. The latter can directly cause anything which is within their power. Thus God, as an omnipotent voluntary cause, can produce any effect whatsoever without acting through the usual secondary causes. Although such an effect may be outside the usual course of nature and contrary to some particular aspect of the object involved, it is not therefore contrary to nature as a whole. For God, as cause of every existent, is the first measure of the essence and nature of every creature. Whatever he makes them be is natural for them. We call a miracle any such event which sometimes occurs and which is beyond the established order of things. Obviously then, only God can make a miracle, but he can produce one either directly or by working through creatures.

MORAL LAW

As creator of the universe God directs all things to their various ends. But he achieves this in different ways. He controls irrational creatures by instilling in them natural inclinations whereby they seek what is good for their species. To men, however, he gives the moral law by which he guides them in their personal conduct. This he does because, having intellect, will and freedom, they can participate in divine providence by controlling themselves and the rest of nature, law being nothing but a certain plan and rule of how to act. The purpose of any law, however, is to direct men to the end intended by the legislator.

The end, however, which God intends is necessarily himself. The divine law has then as its main purpose to direct men to God, to make them more similar to him, which entails making them more perfect and happy.

MAIN PRECEPTS

Since the law's main purpose is to make men adhere to God, and since we can do this most firmly through love, its principal precept must be to love God. This is so because we can adhere to God through our intellect and our will, and the adherence achieved through intellectual knowledge is completed through love, in which the will rests satisfied in the object known. Likewise we could argue that the function of the law is to make men good. A man is good, however, insofar as he has a good will, and the will is good to the extent that it tends to the highest good. Hence the main precept of the moral law must be to love the highest good, namely, God. As a corollary to this precept there follows another, that we must also love our fellow men. For, having all the same end, we should be united to achieve it by bonds of mutual sympathy and affection. Moreover, since we are by nature social animals, we need the help of others to attain our ends. But help is best rendered out of mutual love. Furthermore, the knowledge and love of God require peace and quiet. It is, however, especially through mutual love of each other that we can put up with what disturbs our lives. Hence fraternal charity is another main precept.

TRUE FAITH

There are a number of other precepts of the moral law that we can formulate. One concerns the obligation of seeking for the true faith. Just as we can know the physical world through our senses, so we can know intimately in this life what God is only through faith in what he has revealed. If, then, there are reasonable grounds to believe that a divine revelation has occurred, there would be a corresponding obligation to accept whatever was revealed, even if we cannot understand it completely. Then too, as creatures we are completely the subordinates of God. In regard to the will this is manifested by love; in regard to the intellect, by faith-not, however, by faith in anything false. But God would never propose any error that we should accept.

WORSHIP

Because it is connatural to us to know through our senses, but difficult to transcend such knowledge, we have to use sensible things in such a way as to help us raise our minds to God. Consequently, the sacrifice of physical goods was instituted, not with the idea that God needed them but in order to remind us that we should refer all things to him as our end, creator and ruler. Similarly, other actions like prostration, genuflexion and singing are used, not as though they could affect God, but to help direct our attention to him. For we know by experience that we can through physical acts like these excite ourselves to greater attention and affection. The performance of such acts to bring us closer to God is what is meant by the cult of God. We also call it religion because by it we are attached to God, and etymologically religion refers to being bound. Other synonyms for worship are piety and latria.

PROPER OBJECT OF WORSHIP

Given the purpose of worship, if there is only one creative source for all things in the world, it would be irrational to proffer worship to any other being except him. We must then reject as errors the views often held in the past that worship should be rendered to angels, demons, the souls of the dead and idols. This does not mean of course that we may not honor in other ways those beings that are superior to us, without being divine.

PROPER USE OF PHYSICAL GOODS

Just as the moral law enjoins us to use the things of this world properly, to assimilate ourselves to God, so conversely it must forbid any contrary use of them: the substitution of any of them in the place of God as our ultimate end or the concentration on any of them to such an extent that we are unduly detracted from thinking of him. To put it another way, just as our minds should be subject to God, so should our body to the soul and our inferior powers to our reason. They err, then, who claim that we can do wrong only by hurting or scandalizing our fellow men.

Comment

This last point illustrates how contemporary Thomas can be. One of the main principles of the proponents of the "New Morality" of the 1960's is that we must judge the morality of our acts solely on the basis of how they reflect our interpersonal relations.

REGULATION OF SEX

On this basis it is clear how wrong is the opinion of those who claim that simple fornication is not wrong. They reason that if an unattached adult woman willingly sleeps with a man, he has done no wrong to her or anybody else, and so no sin was committed. It would be insufficient, says Thomas, merely to object that an injury is thereby done to God or that others may be scandalized. Rather, we should remember that what God wants is that each should attain what is good for him. The good of anything, however, consists in attaining its end, while evil is whatever detracts one from his end. Now, the end of the sex act is the generation of children. But since the mere production of offspring without their education would be unreasonable, the sex act should be done only under conditions suitable for the generation and education of children. Hence any way of performing the sex act which would in itself go against these ends would be wrong, although there would be no sin if generation did not result because of some incidental concomitant condition such as sterility. It is also obvious that the human mother is by herself incapable of supporting her children, since so many things have to be provided over a number of years. It is therefore necessary that parents remain together not merely for the physical good of the child, but also so that the firm hand of a father will always be available for the necessary correction of the children. Such a natural society formed by a given man and woman to raise children thus has to be an enduring one. We call it matrimony. Any use of sex outside of it would be against a human good and therefore wrong. Since the semen is provided man for the conservation of the species, any misuse of it is a serious evil. Indeed, it is to be reckoned as only second to murder in its destructiveness of human life. It is thus clear that all coitus except with one's mate is illicit.

INDIVISIBILITY OF MARRIAGE

It is further manifest that matrimony should be not only enduring but for one's whole life. The natural solicitude of parents for their children would require it. But its dissolution would besides entail injustice. It is hard for a woman after she has passed the prime of her life to find a husband. If, then, a woman has expended her youth, beauty and fecundity for her husband, it would certainly be iniquitous to dismiss her. Then, too, since women are naturally subject to their husbands, it would not be in their power to divorce their husbands. If, however, men had this power, marriage would not be a society of equals but would on the contrary be a sort of servitude for the women. So divorce can be permitted to neither. Then too, divorce would be contrary to the good of the children. And of course if divorce were permitted, this would in itself encourage the breaking up of families, while if it is not allowed couples work harder at making their union work.

POLYGAMY

Similar reasons make it clear that marriage should only be between one man and one woman. Polygamy is wrong because one man cannot adequately help a number of wives to rear their children, because it tends, as we know from experience, to the degradation of the women and because it makes impossible the proper and equal love and affection of the mates. Polyandry is wrong for these same reasons, but is worse because it besides makes it impossible to know who the father of the children is.

THE PROPER USE OF DRINK

Just as sexual activity is without sin if done according to reason, the same holds for the use of liquor. Now the reasonable use of anything consists of employing it in accord with its end. The purpose of drink, however, is the conservation of the body through nutrition. Whatever drink serves this purpose can be taken without sin. Drink, however, can be abused, as when too much is taken, or a sort that is injurious to health.

JUSTICE

We should in everything seek to maintain a rational order. Now because man is by nature a social being, one of the most important aspects of his life is his relations with his fellow men. These, then, must be conducted on a rational basis. This entails that we help each other to achieve a fuller possession of truth and to encourage each other to do good and avoid evil. We could put it in another way: every man should play his cosmic role to the hilt. However, to maintain the proper order and concord among men, it is necessary that everyone render to the other his due, which is what we mean by being just. Justice may be manifested in many ways. Thus justice demands that we honor our parents, that we do not hurt or kill our neighbor, that we neither seduce his wife nor steal his property, that we not lie about him nor even desire to take anything he has. Men should voluntarily try to maintain such an order out of love for God and fellow men. For the people who are not disposed to do this on their own, laws and punishments must be provided to ensure their cooperation.

INTRINSIC MORALITY

From what we have seen it is clear that the things enjoined by the divine law are wrong or right not just because the law enjoins them but by their very nature. For by the divine law, men are subjected to God and all other things to men, according to reason. But this is what the natural order of things requires, that the inferior be subject to the superior. Furthermore, God has provided man with reason as a part of his natural equipment to guide his activities. Such a natural function, however, is correlative to the order of nature. What it discovers to be naturally suitable for man to do is right by its very nature, in itself, and not merely because it is ordained by a positive law. Then, too, whatever is necessary to any part of nature is itself natural. But it is clear that man is by nature a social animal, since a man cannot all by himself get all that is necessary for an adequate life. Whatever then is necessary to maintain society is naturally suitable to man and is by nature right. And these are the kinds of things that are also enjoined by the positive moral law.

COUNSELS OF PERFECTION

As we have seen, man's supreme good consists in assimilation to God. It is, however, impossible for us to be intensely preoccupied with a number of affairs. To show us how we can free ourselves from terrestrial concerns so as better to attend to higher matters, the moral law also provides certain indications to this effect. These are called counsels to contrast them with the precepts. We are obliged to follow the latter, but we do no evil if we choose not to practice the former. The three main counsels correspond to the major areas of common human solicitude: our spiritual life (our thoughts and desires), our married life and our economic life. To do away with our solicitude over exterior things we have the counsel of poverty: to give up the possession or use of whatever is not strictly necessary for a life devoted to the pursuit of God. To do away with the distractions resulting from marriage we have the counsel of complete continence. To do away with excessive preoccupations over ourselves we have the counsel of obedience, by which we subject ourselves to the rule of another. The practice of these counsels does not in itself constitute perfection. It simply makes it easier for us to achieve it. As these counsels help us to adhere to God, those who follow them are called religious.

DEGREES OF GOODNESS AND EVIL

From this it is clear that good acts do not all have the same moral value, and the same is true for sins. Thus the religious life is in itself of a higher sort than the married. One reason for these differences of goodness and evil is that the value of any action is determined by that which the act is concerned with. Since we can act for a variety of objects, and since these do not all bring us equally close to our ultimate end, these objects and their corresponding actions have to vary in regard to their goodness. Likewise some sins are a greater perversion of the moral order than others. As a result we must distinguish between mortal and venial sins. A mortal sin is one that involves a rejection of God as our ultimate end and as the ultimate object of our love. Any lesser deficiency in our actions is a venial sin.

DIVINE PUNISHMENTS AND REWARDS

Legislators in general always provide rewards and punishments to encourage the observance of the law. Thus it pertains to divine providence to do likewise. Moreover, it is necessary that he do so since it would be inconsistent with the perfection of his providence to leave any loose ends in his creation. As, however, there are differences in the moral value of acts, so there will be a corresponding variety of rewards and punishments, as is also required by the perfection of the divine justice. Thus the supreme punishment is never to achieve our ultimate end, which is the penalty for mortal sins. This is reasonable since mortal sin consists in the rejection of God as our end. This punishment will last eternally, because after a man has left this life he no longer has the means of acquiring his ultimate end, as he needs his body to do that. Some have argued that any penalty which God would impose would bring about a rehabilitation and so would eventually end. This, however, is not the case, because the rewards and punishments which God gives have to be proportioned to the acts we have performed, and mortal sins are such as to require eternal punishment. Even if we granted that the divine punishments were purgative, this would not prevent them from being without end, because even human laws sometimes impose the death penalty, not, obviously, to rehabilitate the condemned person, but to deter others who might be tempted to commit the same crimes.

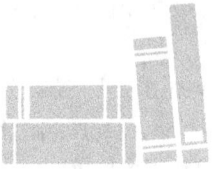

SUMMA THEOLOGICA

TEXTUAL ANALYSIS

PART I

SIGNIFICANCE OF THE SUMMA

Why would anyone nowadays want to read the *Summa Theologica*? The basic reason is that it gives some of the profoundest answers yet to man's theological and philosophical problems. Thus many people study it for theological purposes, since the Roman Catholic church recognizes Thomas as its foremost theologian. Most readers, however, are interested in it mainly for its philosophy. They will therefore skip the more theological sections. But why did Thomas combine theology and philosophy in this way? Partly, it was the custom of his age. Mostly, it was because of the very nature of his task. Theology is an explanation of divine revelation, but as such it bases itself on some philosophy. Since Thomas was dissatisfied with the Augustinian philosophy that was current in his day, in developing his theology he also had to present its philosophical underpinnings. The latter does not therefore depend on the former, and many people have adopted Thomas' philosophy without accepting his theology.

ORGANIZATION

Part I of the *Summa* deals in general with God and his creation. But before one starts it, he should know the breakdown and order of its topics. They are grouped as follows. The upper case headings indicate the areas with a greater philosophical interest, which we will concentrate on.

The Summa

Q. 1 Nature Of Theology

QQ. 2 -11 God's Existence And Nature

QQ. 12-13 Our Knowledge Of God

QQ. 14-26 The Divine Operations

QQ. 27-43 The Trinity

QQ. 44-50 Creation And Distinction Of Things

QQ. 51-64 The Angels

QQ. 65-74 The Creation of the World

QQ. 75-89 The Nature Of Man

QQ. 90-102 The First Man

QQ. 103-119 God's Governance Of The World

QUESTIONS 2-11: GOD'S EXISTENCE AND NATURE

The Existence Of God

Some statements, like "2 + 2 = 4," are self-evident. As soon as you understand what the terms mean, you immediately see that it has to be true. The statement "God exists" can never be self-evident for us, since we have neither an intuition of God's nature nor any direct experience of him, which we would need to make that statement self-evident.

Comment

This point would seem obvious to most people, but some philosophers have denied it. Among them is St. Anselm (1033-1109), who in his famous "ontological argument" sought to show how the existence of God is analytic. His view was the one that Thomas especially had in mind. Some modern philosophers, like Descartes and Leibniz, have defended other versions of the ontological argument.

Since it is not self-evident that God exists, we must prove it. The only way to do this is to show that the things of this world are necessarily the effects of a cause, which therefore exists and which we call God.

> Comment

In raising this point Thomas was striking against those thinkers who held that we can know only through faith that God exists. There are still such people. Nowadays, however, the most common objections against it are made by Kantians and naturalists. The former maintain that causality can be used validly to connect together the objects of our experience, but not to infer the existence of an object outside of our experience. The latter hold that there exist only those entities which can be investigated by the empirical sciences. Thomas would answer both by showing that the principle of causality is universal, that it applies to all beings, and so can be used to learn about things which we cannot directly experience.

Thomas then gives his celebrated Five Ways of proving that there is a God. The first: things are continually moving (changing), but this is possible only if there is ultimately a first, unmoved mover, called God. The second: various things are presently causing others to be while they are at the same time being caused by others; but such a series of causes and effects, each of which is simultaneously dependent on a prior cause, is possible only if there is a first, uncaused cause, which we call God. The third: we find a certain necessity in things: they have to be what they are, but since they are not necessary of themselves they have to receive their necessity ultimately from a being that is necessary in itself and that is the source of the necessity of all the others, which being is called God. The fourth: things exist in different degrees of perfection, but since whatever has a lower degree of perfection received it ultimately from a source which is the perfection to the highest degree, there is a supremely perfect being, called God, who is the cause of whatever perfections other beings have. The fifth: even the inanimate things of this world act in an ordered, purposeful way, but since they cannot do this of themselves there has to be an intelligent being, which we call God, that directs them to their end.

Comment

The Five Ways are so elliptical that they obviously were not meant as complete, formal proofs for the existence of God. They merely indicate in general five ways one can proceed to work out such proofs. The actual working out of them Thomas here left to the reader. Our bibliography mentions various books which expand and explain in detail the Five Ways. Note that they are all variations of one basic, causal argument: given effects of a certain type which are being produced right now, there must at the same time exist an ultimate absolute cause which is producing them through the intermediary of various secondary causes. The Five Ways are much more meaningful if read in conjunction with the formal proof for God's existence which Thomas gives in Chapter Five of *On Being and Essence*.

The Divine Essence

Thomas' understanding of what fundamentally constitutes God's nature can be seen through a comparison of the conclusions of the Five Ways with those of the *Summa Contra Gentiles* (I, ch. 22). There he speaks of a "sublime truth": the very existence of God is his essence. In other words, God's essence and existence are identical. His essence is simply to exist. He is the pure act of existing. As such then he has no potency for any movement or change, but can cause it, and so is the first, unmoved mover and uncaused cause. Since he is being itself, he is the only thing that is absolutely necessary; that is, necessary in itself. Since he is the sheer actuality of existence, he is supremely perfect and the source of any lesser perfection. Thus, he is also the supreme intelligence which directs all things to their ends.

Comment

Thomas has what is called an existentialist notion of the nature of God, as contrasted with the essentialist idea of most other philosophers. The latter hold that the essence of God is to be a certain kind of being, for example, an absolutely perfect or infinite being. Thomas holds that God is not some kind of being, but that he is being itself. Note again that Thomas is an existentialist in a completely different sense than a contemporary thinker like Sartre.

God's Simplicity: In this context simplicity means the lack of parts, of constitutive factors. All creatures consist of combinations of actual and potential factors. Thus a physical body is composed of prime matter (pure potency), substantial form and various accidental forms; a pure spirit like an angel is a quiddity which is in potency to existence. Bodies then have a rather complicated **metaphysical** structure; that of spirits is simpler; but God's is absolutely simple because, being pure act, there is no potency whatsoever in him. We can in our own minds distinguish between his quiddity and existence but in him they are simply identical. They have to be absolutely the same in God, because if they were different there would have to be some external, prior cause to make them cohere. But God is the first, uncaused cause.

Perfection Of God

Something is perfect when it has everything that it should. Perfection then corresponds to actuality. As the first cause, God is pure act and thus supremely perfect. The various perfections we find in creatures, since they were caused by God, necessarily exist in him, but in a more perfect manner. Indeed, since God is the pure act of existence, and since any perfection is simply a certain mode of existing, God then possesses to the fullest degree every possible perfection. Creatures are similar to God to the extent that they share in a limited manner the perfections which God is in an unlimited fashion and in accordance with his simplicity.

Goodness In General

A thing is good insofar as it can be the goal of a desire. But it can satisfy a desire only to the extent that its, perfection or actuality will allow. But since being is the actuality of all else, a thing is good only insofar as it has being. Thus being and goodness are really the same thing, although conceptually they differ. Goodness is being, considered as desirable. The notion of being, then, is necessarily had before that of goodness, and every being is good, according to the degree of its actuality. As a result the good acts as a telic or final cause. By being desirable it causes the action of the one seeking it. We may distinguish three kinds. The useful good is whatever is desired as a means to a further good. The autonomous good is that which is wanted for itself. The delectable good is the satisfaction one gets from the possession of the desired object.

God's Goodness

We should associate goodness with God above all since he is the highest good. He is such absolutely, not just in a relative way. As he is being itself, he is the first cause of whatever else is desirable, that is, good. Any created good is thus merely a limited reflection of his goodness. But creatures merely have goodness. God is goodness itself since he is being itself, and goodness is simply being considered as desirable.

God's Infinity

To be infinite means to be without limitation. Whenever any actuality or perfection is restricted, this is because it has been circumscribed by being received into some potency. The source or principle of limitation is always potency, because actuality of itself is perfection and as such does not limit itself. But God is the pure act of existence. Therefore no potency restricts his being, and he is then infinite. Only God is infinite in the absolute sense, although other things are said to be infinite in a qualified sense. Thus, any material object is actually what it is and nothing else, but potentially it is an infinite number of other things. Nor could the physical universe be said to be actually infinite in size. For every physical reality has a determinate quantity which can be either smaller or greater. Likewise, no number is actually infinite. But from the point of view of its potentiality a number may be infinite insofar as it can be added to indefinitely.

God's Omnipresence

God's infinity would seem to entail that he is everywhere and in everything, and this is indeed the case. God is present in all things not as part of their substance or as an accident but through his causal activity. God not only starts things in their existence, but he is what is continually causing them to remain in existence as long as they do. Thus, since being is what is most basic to any object and God is always causing it, he is present in the most basic and intimate way in all objects. Thus, he is everywhere. For place exists only inasmuch as there are things to fill it. So, since God is in every object he is thereby in every place. Further, he is in all things in a three-fold manner: by his power, since all things are subject to it; by his knowledge, since nothing is hidden from him; and by his essence, since he causes their very being. Only God then is primarily and essentially omnipresent, because only he is wholly present in every place.

God's Immutability

That God is unchanging can be shown in several ways. Since change is the going from a potential to an actual state, God, being pure act without any potency, is incapable of changing. Again, when something changes it remains in part what it was while becoming in part something different, so it has parts; but God is simple, that is, he has no parts, and hence he cannot change. Then too, whatever changes acquires something it lacked; but since God is infinite he lacks nothing and so cannot change. Only God is absolutely immutable. All of his creatures are subject to one or another type of change. Corporeal beings are subject to substantial change; the apple when eaten becomes a part of the eater. Spiritual beings, on the other hand, undergo only accidental changes: they may come to know more deeply or love more firmly. This is because both corporeal and spiritual beings are composed of act and potency, while only God is pure act.

Comment

In this question as in many others, Thomas uses examples from the science of his day, which we now realize to be seriously deficient and often erroneous. Although some of his examples may thus no longer be very persuasive, the student should not let this obscure the philosophic validity of the underlying argument.

God's Eternity

Boethius (470-525), in his *On the Consolation of Philosophy*, defined eternity well in saying it is the simultaneously whole and perfect possession of unending life. To see that this is right, we must remember that we arrive at the notion of eternity by first knowing what time is. In this changing world there is a continual succession of events which we can number according to whether they come before or after each other. This numerability of changing, successive things is precisely what we mean by time. Whatever then exists temporally has a beginning and end in time. But by the eternal we mean the contrary of the temporal; we mean what is simultaneously whole, that is, without any change or beginning or end. It is also said to be the possession of unending life, rather than existence, to show that God is not inert but active. Since God is living and immutable, he is then also eternal. Indeed he is his own eternity. In contrast to this, no other being is its own duration, because none is its own being. Only God then is fully and properly eternal, as only he is absolutely unchanging. We must, however, be careful not to think of time as merely a part of eternity, as do those who hold that time consists merely of having a beginning and end, while eternity does not. That is just an accidental difference. The real difference lies in that eternity refers to an unchanging existence, whereas time has to do with a changing one. Eternity then is different from both aeviternity and time. For, eternity measures completely unchanging existence. Time measures existence that is subject to radical, substantial change. Aeviternity measures being that is accompanied only by accidental change, which condition is found in the angels.

God's Unity

In the same way that goodness is simply being considered in its desirability, so oneness or unity is being considered as forming an undivided whole. Thus, the various parts which make up a car are not said to be a unity until a mechanic has put them all together. Unity and the one are then the opposites of multiplicity and the many. That there is only one God can be shown from his infinite perfection. If we accept the impossible hypothesis that there are two infinitely perfect beings, this entails that they are different in some way, otherwise they would be one, not two. One then would lack something that the other has and so would not be perfect. Thus it is inconceivable that there is more than one infinite being, that is, more than one God. There are, however, various degrees of unity. Thus, the more parts an object has, the weaker does its unity tend to be. God then is one to the highest degree. For since there is only a logical distinction between unity and being, the more perfect being will have the more perfect unity. As God is the most perfect being, he is therefore the most perfect unity. We could also prove this another way. Unity refers to the lack of division. But God, because of his absolute simplicity, is the only being who is not divided in any way, either potentially or actually. He is therefore absolutely and to the highest degree one.

QQ. 12-13: OUR KNOWLEDGE OF GOD

How God Is Known By Us

Since God is incorporeal, we cannot know him through the senses but only through the intellect. In this life, however, we can never come to a direct knowledge of the divine essence, because now we are limited to knowing sensible objects and what we can infer from such knowledge. On this basis we can know that God exists, that certain predicates necessarily belong to him since he is the cause of all things, but also that he is immeasurably greater than any of them. Such knowledge is natural to us but is less perfect than what we can have when God grants us special revelations or aid. This natural knowledge has three moments. First we recognize God as cause of the universe. Next we see that any defect or limitation found in creatures could not belong to him. Then we affirm of him to the highest degree any pure perfection that we find in a limited way in creatures.

How We Speak About God

We use words to express our thoughts, and thoughts are likenesses of things. Hence what we say refers to objects only indirectly, through our thoughts. The language by which we refer to God is even more indirect, however, as we know about him only as an inference from objects. Can we then say anything about him that is really meaningful, that will express what he himself is? The problem here is not about negative terms like immutability, which tell only what God is not, or relational terms like cause. It is whether terms like good and wise really say anything about him. Some say no. Thus Moses Maimonides held that all such terms are really negative; for instance, to say that God is alive means only that he is not similar to inanimate objects. Others say that such terms are merely relational; for instance, to say that God is good means only that he is the cause of goodness in things. Such views, however, are untenable because they cannot explain why certain terms are applied to God but not others and because they misinterpret what people mean to say by such statements. Rather, such terms when applied to God really say what he is, even though they express it imperfectly. Thus, to say that God is good means that goodness such as is found in creatures also exists in God but in a far superior manner. Such terms do express perfections that are in God, although their creaturely **connotations** are inappropriate. Nor can it be said that these words are merely synonyms, because although they all refer to the same one being they represent different aspects of him.

Analogical Character Of Theological Language

Words are of three types: univocal, equivocal and analogous. A univocal term is one that is always used in exactly the same sense. But when we predicate a term of God we are always using it differently than when we predicate it of a creature, because we always affirm it of him in a transcendent and pre-eminent way. Thus theological language cannot be univocal. An equivocal term is one that is used to mean essentially different things. Thus, "bank" is equivocal when used to refer to a place for money and to the side of a river. We cannot then use purely equivocal terms to speak about God, because such statements would be simply meaningless. Analogical terms stand for objects or aspects that are essentially different but have some similarity or connection.

Thus the qualities in a mother and a steak which make us call them both good are essentially different, but similar insofar as they refer to proper performance of functions. Good is therefore an analogical term. The only way we can talk about God is by using such words, because we necessarily conceive of God in terms of the physical objects and modalities which make up our experience of this world. We affirm of God the same predicates that we do of objects, realizing all the while that these terms mean something essentially different though somewhat similar or related in either case. When words are used analogically, the problem arises as to which analogue is primary. When the analogy is metaphorical (God is a lion), the analogous term has its primary meaning in the creature. In all other cases, however, the analogous predicate is found primarily in God and only secondarily in creatures, because they exist in the most perfect manner in God, while in creatures they manifest themselves only in a limited, participated fashion. This is true even though we first understand the meaning of such words in their application to creatures.

QQ. 14-26: THE DIVINE OPERATIONS

God's Knowing

God knows in the most full and perfect sense. To understand this we must keep in mind what knowledge is and what makes it possible. To know is to possess the form of another without its matter. A being then that can know is less limited than one that cannot. The principle of all limitation, however, is potentiality, and in the case of physical objects it is prime matter, which is pure potentiality. The basis of all knowledge then is immateriality or freedom from the limitations imposed by potency. Thus plants cannot know because they are limited to having their own forms only. Brutes are capable of some knowledge because they are not so restricted but can through their senses take on the accidental forms of objects. Man has an even greater cognitive power, because his intellect is so free of restrictions that it can become all things. But since God is pure act, with no potency whatsoever, he is immaterial to the highest degree and so can know most fully and perfectly. It might be thought that God does not know himself, because as we experience knowledge in ourselves it is the actualization by objects of our senses or intellect, which are in potency to the forms of these objects. Since there is no potency in God, it might seem then that there can be no knowing either. But this is not the case. Because God is purely actual and simple, the divine intellect and what it knows are identical in every way, and so God knows himself perfectly through himself. Moreover, his very act of knowing, his intellect, his object of knowledge, his substance and his existence are all the same. For if they were distinct, one would be in potency to the other, and there is no potency in him. From this it follows that God necessarily knows things other than himself. For included in his perfect knowledge of himself is the understanding of whatever he is capable of. But since he is the first cause of everything that is or may be, he therefore knows them all. And just as he knows himself in himself, so also he knows all things other than himself, not in themselves, but in himself, because they are only copies of his ideas of them.

A problem arises here as to whether this knowledge of other things is only general or perfect in every detail. But the same reasoning would hold. Since he causes them in every detail, likewise must he so know them. This knowledge, moreover, is in no way discursive. Ours is, insofar as we know one thing after another, and insofar as the knowledge of one thing is the cause of our knowledge of others. God's knowledge cannot be discursive in the first way because, as we have seen, he knows all things in himself and therefore simultaneously. Neither can it be discursive in the second way, because besides presupposing the first way it would involve God in a change - from ignorance to knowledge - and he is immutable. God's knowledge is also the cause of things. Just as the knowledge of an artist when conjoined with a will to produce is the cause of a work of art, so it is that God's knowledge causes things when united with a willing thereto.

What God Knows

God necessarily knows everything that exists in any way whatsoever. Things exist in diverse ways. Besides those that are actually existing, others exist potentially, in creatures or in God himself, as powers or as mental products. In this sense God knows even nonexistent beings that will never exist except as possibilities. Likewise then, he also knows evil. Since he knows everything perfectly, he necessarily knows whatever happens to anything. Thus, when an object is deprived of some good, he also knows it in this state of deprivation. He thereby knows evil, which is only the privation of some good in an object which should have it. That is, he knows evils by knowing the otherwise good beings in which these evils exist. It also follows that his knowledge is infinite: there is no end to the number of different individual things that he knows down to every detail.

Future Contingent Events

Since God knows all things, he therefore knows all future contingent events too. A contingent event is one that is not necessary, that need not happen. If a contingent event has occurred we can know it with certitude. If it has not yet occurred, then we have no way of knowing for sure whether it will or not. This is because we know contingent events only one after another as they occur. God, however, does not know them like this, in succession, but all at once, simultaneously. God, being eternal, includes the whole of time in his knowledge, but the temporal succession of events he sees all at once as an eternal present. Thus, what is for us a contingent event of the future is for God in the present, and he knows it just as easily as we know present contingent events.

The Divine Ideas

The word "idea" comes from the Greek and it means form. The idea or form of an object considered as existing outside of that object can have two functions. It can serve either as the archetype of that object or to make the object known. For knowledge is the possession of the form of another but without its matter. Since God is the cause of this universe, which is such an orderly complex, he necessarily has an idea of it whereby he makes and knows it. Since, as we have seen, God knows himself and all other things by contemplating his own essence, his ideas and his essence are simply identical. That he has many different ideas is clear, since he causes many diverse objects. Now, this is not incompatible with the divine simplicity. It would be incompatible if he possessed ideas like men do, as causal entities distinct from each other. But God's ideas, though different from each other, are not distinct causes of God's knowing. What "causes" God to know is his essence, which is one, and which, being existence itself, he sees to be imitable in various ways. These infinitely varying aspects of the divine being considered as the archetypes of things are the divine ideas. Thus God has ideas of all things that exist or are possible. Nevertheless, we cannot say that he has ideas of such negations as evil. But this is because evil is not a being but a lack of being. He knows an evil in his idea of an object that is good but is suffering from an undue limitation.

Comment

Plato (427-348 B. C.) had earlier conceived of "Ideas" as the archetypes of the objects of this world. But for him these Ideas, which were universal, infinite, perfect and immutable forms, did not exist in any mind, not even God's. They simply subsisted eternally by themselves. The Demiurge (God) used them as patterns to make the individual, corporeal copies of them that we see about us. These objects are thus participation in the Ideas. Aristotle rejected both the theory of the Ideas and of participation on the grounds that self-subsisting Ideas were impossible. St. Augustine (354-430), however, adopted Plato's views while modifying them, maintaining that the ideas were not self-subsisting but had existed eternally in the mind of God. Thomas follows Augustine, but his view of God's nature introduces important differences.

Truth In General

Just as the good is what satisfies desire, the true is what satisfies the intellect. However, there is a difference in that goodness is in the desired object whereas truth is in the knower. But just as goodness is the relation of desirability on the part of an object to an appetite, so truth is the relation of conformity between an intellect and an object. Although truth is predicated primarily of the intellect, the object it knows is also called true because of its relation to this intellect. The known object, however, can be related to intellect either essentially or incidentally. Objects are essentially related to the divine intellect because they exist only insofar as they are known by it. They are related incidentally to the human intellect by which they may happen to be known. In general, then, truth may be defined as the equation of object and intellect. It is clear too that a thing is knowable only insofar as it exists, and vice versa. The reason is that truth, like goodness, is only logically distinct from being. For truth is simply being, considered as knowable, just as goodness is being, considered as appetible.

God Is The Highest Truth

As we have seen, truth is in the intellect insofar as it understands things as they are. It is in objects to the extent that they conform to an intellect. It is found in both ways to the highest degree in God. Not only is his being conformed to his intellect, it is his very act of knowing. Indeed, in him his intellect, his act of knowing and his being are simply identical. And they are also the cause of every other being and intellect. Thus, not only is there truth in him, but he is himself the highest and first truth.

God Is Life

We can understand the difference between living and nonliving things by considering some which are obviously alive: the animals. We judge them to be alive when they start to move themselves. We say they have lost their life and are dead when they can no longer move themselves but must be moved by others. To be alive then is to move oneself in any way. Such self-movement may be an action like walking or it may be an operation like thinking or sensing. The latter are also said analogically to be actions and movements because they are the perfection of the being acting, just as any movement is the perfection of a potentiality. To live, then, is to be in a certain manner, in such a way as to be capable of self-movement, and life means simply this kind of existence. However, life is sometimes also used to mean the operations of a living being. But life has various levels of perfection, depending on how fully autonomous it is. The lowest level of life is that of plants, which perform certain actions but only in accord with the precise patterns and end ordained by their nature. The next level of life is that of the brutes, whose actions are all for an end ordained by their nature but whose pattern of action varies according to their reaction to what they perceive. A higher level yet is found among men, who choose their own ends and vary their actions accordingly. But even men are determined to a certain extent from the outside. For instance, they must, by their nature, tend toward the good. The highest form of life would then consist in complete autonomy, in receiving no determination whatsoever from the outside. But this is found only in God, so he is in the fullest sense life.

God's Willing

All things tend to act according to their nature. Thus, when men apprehend some good through their intellect, they have a natural tendency to seek it if they do not have it and to continue loving it after they have achieved it. They do this through the power we call the will. Since God also has intellectual knowledge, there will be in him something analogous to the will. But just as his knowing is identical with his being, so is his willing. Besides this, all beings tend to share with others the goodness they possess. This would then be especially the case with the divine will. Thus God wills that both he and other things exist. But he wills himself as the ultimate good; others, only as ordered to himself. It follows therefore that some things he necessarily wills, but not others.

We should distinguish, however, between absolute and hypothetical necessity. Since God is the perfect good, he wills with an absolute necessity only himself. When he wills other things it is at most with a hypothetical necessity: if he wills X, he must also will whatever makes X possible. God's will is thus the cause of everything besides himself and it is free, that is, not determined by anything outside of himself. Thus too, whatever he wills, necessarily occurs. If it is not achieved in one way, it will be in another. This is not to deny that contingent and free events occur. They do. But it would be false to say that events are contingent simply because they are produced by contingent causes, because this would imply that such causes are removed from God's knowledge and will. Rather we should say that God wills certain things to occur necessarily and others contingently. For the former he sets up causes such that their effects cannot be prevented. For the latter he sets up defectible, contingent causes from which effects proceed only contingently. So, whatever occurs, necessarily occurs as God wills, as necessary or contingent effects. In other words, contingent effects have a hypothetical necessity. However, we cannot say that God wills evil as such, although he may will it incidentally. An evil is the lack of a good which should be present. As such, it can be the object of no appetite. Inasmuch, however, as it can "exist" only in a larger good, such a defective good can be desired for the good that it contains, and thus in an incidental manner the defect is willed at the same time. Thus by willing justice God wills the physical evils which result as things change. In no way, however, does God will the evil of sin, since it is a negation of the divinely established order.

God's Providence

As we have seen, God is the cause of every being and good in the world and he causes them through his intellect and will. But the very order of the world is a great good which likewise had to preexist in God's mind. This plan by which things are coordinated to achieve their ends is what we call divine providence. Contrary to those philosophers who would restrict to a greater or lesser degree the scope of God's providence, we must say that everything falls under it, since he is the cause of all things. This is not to deny chance events. But these occur only in relation to a finite series of causes and effects, in which an unexpected event takes place as a result of the interference of a cause from a different series. But there is no such interaction unknown to God.

Divine Omnipotence

Potency is a ambiguous word as it sometimes means a passive potency or potentiality, which cannot exist in God. Active potency, however, means power, which does exist in God and to the highest degree, since he is pure act. Indeed, because God's being is infinite, his power is too. We commonly express this by saying that God is omnipotent. This, however, is sometimes misinterpreted to mean that God can do anything. What it really means is that he can do anything that is possible. Thus, whatever involves an internal contradiction, like a "square circle," is simply not possible. It is better therefore to say simply that such a thing cannot be made, rather than that God cannot make it. For the same reason we cannot say that God could make the past not to be. Some men have argued, however, that he can do only what he actually does do, that he is determined to one course of action because of his supreme wisdom, which knows it as the best. This argument might be valid if God's action were ordered necessarily to one definite, limited end. But this is not the case. The end of his actions is his own infinite goodness, and so he can will to share it in an infinite variety of ways. Thus he could have made a better world than this.

The Happiness Of God

Happiness is the realization of the sufficiency of a possessed good. But since God is the perfection of being and intelligence, he is happy to the utmost degree. It is clear that, by its very nature, happiness is the highest good of any intellectual nature. And since the most perfect operation of an intellectual nature is its act of understanding, this is what happiness primarily consists in. It might be objected that since happiness is something desired, it is therefore the object of the will, and thus God's happiness would reside primarily in the satisfaction of his will. Granted that happiness is the object of the will. But for the will to possess it, it must first exist, which it does only in the intellect. Thus all happiness is primarily intellectual and only secondarily a matter of the will.

QQ. 44-50: CREATION AND DIVERSITY OF THINGS

What Kind Of A Cause Is God?

We have seen that God is the first efficient cause of all things since he is being itself, and all other things exist only insofar as he makes them participate in diverse ways and degrees in his existence. Some philosophers, like Plato, however, thought that although God was the cause of all things, he made them out of an uncreated, eternal matter. But this cannot be. Since God makes things to exist, he necessarily causes them completely. He is also the exemplary cause of all things inasmuch as they are all reflections of his ideas of them. He is the telic or final cause (end, purpose) of all things too. When God acts, he is his own end, but he is not seeking to add anything to himself, only to share his perfection with his creatures. Whereas when a creature acts, it is always seeking for itself a further perfection, which is only a higher participation in the divine goodness. In this way God is the end of every activity.

Creation

To create is to produce completely, without any raw material whatsoever. We often say that an artist is a creator. This is not strictly true, since he does not make his canvas or granite. Because, however, God is the cause of absolutely everything outside of himself, he had to produce them out of nothing, something only he can do. It was the common opinion among the Greeks that the world was eternal. It is not possible to prove philosophically either that the world had a beginning or that it did not. God could have made the world to be through all eternity, but we know through revelation that he did not. Thus, time and the universe started simultaneously at the moment of creation.

The Diversity Of Creatures

The reasons for which God creates are to share his goodness with his creatures and to manifest it to him. For this, one single creature would not suffice. To manifest all the different aspects of his goodness he had to create many things of various sorts.

Thus the range of his causation runs from the most limited physical object, like a rock, to man, who is partly physical and partly spiritual, to the angels, who are wholly spiritual.

The Nature And Cause Of Evil

Some, like the Pythagoreans, have held that beings are divided into two genera, the good and the evil. However, these are not beings, only contrary predicates affirmed of beings. Any object, insofar as it exists, has some perfection and is therefore desirable and good. Since evil is the opposite of good, the absence of good, we can understand what it is only in terms of the good. But note that it is not the absence of any good that constitutes evil, only the absence of a good that should be present. For instance, it is an evil for a man to lack sight, but not for a rock. Thus, only an object that is otherwise good can be the support of an evil. For this reason we can call the good the material cause of evil. However, evil does not have a formal cause, being itself the negation of form. Likewise it has no telic cause or purpose, being precisely the absence of the required order to an end. Only incidentally does it have an efficient cause, because every activity has for its end a good, not an evil. If an evil does happen to be caused, it is only because the agent missed his mark, being either too strong or too weak, or because the raw material used was deficient. Thus God could be said to be the cause of evil only incidentally.

QQ. 75-93: MAN'S NATURE AND OPERATIONS

Man's Soul

We call some things alive, others not, depending on whether or not they can perform such operations as moving themselves and knowing. The soul is simply the first principle of life, that is, what makes a body alive. Some philosophers, like Democritus, taught that the soul itself was a body. But a body as such cannot be the cause of life, otherwise every body would be alive. A body then is alive only by virtue of some actuality within it, and it is this actuality that is the soul. Unlike the souls of plants and brutes, however, that of man is incorporeal and substantial. We infer this from the fact that men can know all things. If, however, the soul or intellect were corporeal or worked through a corporeal organ, it would not be able to know such a variety of objects. It is thus incorporeal. Moreover, it has operations, like reasoning, which are proper to it and which cannot be caused in it by a body. Since only substances can act by themselves, the soul is one. Some have denied this, because thinking always involves perception and imagination. This, however, does not occur because the intellect uses the body as an organ. Perception simply provides the raw material which the intellect, so to speak, works over.

Some philosophers make no distinction between sensation and understanding and so attribute both of them to the body. Plato did distinguish between them, but he thought that they were both actions of an incorporeal soul and so concluded that the souls of animals were subsistent or substantial too. Aristotle pointed out, however, that the intellect does not need a corporeal organ to operate. On the other hand, the animal soul in its operations of sensation and sense perception requires the body, and so it is no substantial. As a result, for Plato man was only the soul, which happens to be using a body. Aristotle, however, correctly holds that man is the composite of body and soul. Another mistake sometimes made about the soul maintains that it is itself a hylomorphic compound, that it is constituted by a substantial form determining prime matter. This cannot be, because the soul itself is the substantial form of the hylomorphic compound which is the man. Then too, if the soul were composed of matter and form, it could only know singular, material things, like animals do. From all this it follows that although the souls of brutes and plants cease to exist upon the dissolution of the brutes and plants, human souls do not, since they are substantial in their own right.

The Union Of The Soul And The Body

The intellect, which is what enables man to think, is the substantial form of the human body. For the substantial form of anything is that actuality or perfection whereby it primarily is and acts, since a thing acts only to the extent that it has emerged from potency. We call the substantial form of a living body its soul. Thus, all the vital functions found in man, like nutrition, sensation, movement and thinking, stem from his substantial form, whether we prefer to call it his intellect or his intellectual soul. The mode of union between body and soul is among the closest and most direct, being of an act determining its potency. Since it results in a substance, it is called a substantial unity, as opposed to the accidental unity which some philosophers say is all that man has. Thus, Plato held that the soul simply has its abode for a certain time in the body and uses it. It follows too that since every man has his own sensations and thoughts, that each has his own intellect, contrary to Averroes, who taught that there is only one intellect for all men. On the other hand, we must also reject the view that there is more than one soul in one living body. For it is the form that makes a thing exist and be what it is. Thus if a body had two or three souls, it would be two or three different things. So we cannot say, as some did, that there are in man a plant, an animal and a human soul. Nevertheless it is clear that the human soul has within itself all the powers which the lower souls do. Since the soul is the substantial form of the body, it is necessarily throughout every part of the body. Moreover, the whole soul is present in each part according to the totality of its perfection but not of its operations.

The Powers Of The Soul

Some thinkers believe that the soul and its powers are identical, but this is impossible. In the first place, the powers are accidents, since they are potencies to actions which are obviously accidents. But the soul is in the category of substance since it is the substantial form. As accidents are patently different and distinct from the substance in which they inhere, the soul and its powers are distinct. A second way to establish the same conclusion is based on the fact that the soul is actuality, being the substantial form. But if the soul were identical with its powers, since it is actuality it would then be always performing all its operations, which it obviously is not. Now, since the powers are not perceivable by the senses, we can know about them only through the actions to which they are ordered. There will be as many different powers as there are different kinds of actions, since power is to action as potency is to act. Actions, however, differ according to their object, that is, that which causes or is the goal of the action. However, powers and actions are differentiated not on the basis of any diversity found in the object, but only the differences to which the powers are ordered. Thus the power of sight is ordered to color, while to power of hearing is ordered to sound. Hence, whether the colored thing seen is mineral, plant or animal is irrelevant as far as the act of seeing is concerned. All these powers have their source in the soul, but it might be asked whether they inhere in the soul itself or in the composite of soul and body. This will depend on what performs the operations. Since thinking and willing are performed without any physical organs by the soul, the intellect and the will inhere in the soul. All powers connected with activities done with physical organs, like seeing, necessarily have as their subject the body-soul complex. What then happens to these powers when at death body and soul are separated? Since the intellect and will inhere directly in the soul, they will continue to remain with it. Those powers which inhere in the besouled body will cease to actually exist. But since all powers have their source in the soul, they will remain virtually or radically present in the soul.

Types Of Powers And Souls

There are three different kinds of soul and life. The rational soul has some operations so far above the capacities of the body that they are exercised without using any physical organ. Next is the animal soul, whose operations require physical organs but are relatively independent of any physical qualities. The lowest type is the plant soul, which operates through physical organs and under the influence of the body's qualities. There are five genera of powers found in the rational soul: the vegetative, sense, appetitive, motor and intellectual powers. Each genus has various species. Thus among the vegetative are the powers of nutrition, growth and reproduction. These are the only powers plants have. Animals have these plus the senses and sense appetites. Men have all the powers found in the other animals, plus the intellect and will.

The External Senses

Albert the Great, Thomas' teacher, thought that we should differentiate the senses on the basis of their organs. But this would not be proper since different organs exist only insofar as required by the powers and not vice versa. Rather, we must distinguish various senses on the basis of what pertains to each properly and in itself. Each sense is a capacity to be affected by some outer stimulus. There will then be as many different senses as there are irreducibly different kinds of stimuli perceivable. On this basis we can distinguish five external senses: sight, hearing, taste, smell and touch. Note that objects can affect others in two ways, physically and spiritually. The first occurs when an object receives a form from another in such a way as to be physically changed by it, as when one thing is heated by another. The second occurs when an object receives a form from another but without undergoing any physical change, as when in seeing a green wall we receive the form of greenness but without becoming ourselves green physically. Sensation sometimes occurs with only this nonphysical change, sometimes with both types.

The Internal Senses

Besides the external senses, there are found in animals four internal ones. Here again we must distinguish a different power for each irreducibly different type of activity. Thus, the "common" or central sense is the power by which the animal is simultaneously aware of the various forms being known through the external senses, and is able to distinguish them from each other and to unify them into a single perception. The imagination is the power by which these perceptions are retained for future use to know objects which are no longer present. The estimative power enables the animal to know what is useful and harmful to it; for instance, sheep who have never before seen a wolf know on meeting one that it is dangerous. By memory the animal preserves all such knowledge and later uses it with an awareness of it as a past occurrence.

The Intellectual Powers

Although we sometimes speak of man's soul as the intellect, this is only a manner of speaking. Only in God is the intellect identical with his essence. In creatures the intellect is always a power inhering in the substance of the creature. By it man is able to know every kind of being. But it is obvious that man is not always actually knowing them all, as God does. In other words, man's intellect is in potency to the intelligibles, to whatever it can know. As Aristotle said, it is like a clean slate on which nothing is written. Since this is the case, man must be made to know. That is, in the act of understanding, the intellect is passive, in this precise sense, that it is changed from a state of potential to actual knowing by a cause distinct from it.

Some have thought that just as the sense powers are put in act by such sensible forms as color, sound and the like, so the intellect could be put in act directly by the intelligible forms. The two situations, however, are completely different. The sensible forms are in act in the object, whereas the intelligible forms are there only as potential intelligibles. There must be in man another intellectual power, which is in act and is therefore active, which makes the potentially intelligible forms of objects actually so. This it does by freeing the intelligible form from the material conditions which inhibit it from actualizing the passive intellect. We can then with Aristotle compare the active or agent intellect with a searchlight making visible whatever it picks up. The active and the passive are the only two intellectual powers that we have. The passive intellect, however, goes under various names, depending on which function we refer to it. When we consider it as actually knowing, we may call it intelligence. When we consider it as intuitively knowing an essence or forming a judgment, we speak of it as the understanding. When we consider it as going from the knowledge of one truth to another, we refer to it as reason. When we consider it as apprehending truths for their own sake and not to produce something with them, it is known as the speculative intellect. When we consider it as ordering its knowledge to the production of some object or work, we call it the practical intellect.

Appetitive Powers

Knowing and desiring are not the same kind of operations. We know an object insofar as it is an intelligible or sensible being; we desire it, however, insofar as it is good. Knowing and desiring then are done by different powers. Appetitive powers, however, must be stimulated by what is known; hence the kids of appetites will correspond to the kinds of cognitive powers: there are in man both sense and intellectual appetites. There are two sense appetites, the concupiscible or pleasure appetite and the irascible or fighter appetite. They are different because they have different functions. By the concupiscible appetite, we tend toward goods that we perceive to be pleasant and avoid the contrary. By the irascible appetite, we resist whatever threatens us. That they are different powers is also shown by the fact that we sometimes desire by one power what we are rejecting through the other. There is, however, in man only one intellectual appetite, which we call the will, and to which the sense appetites are subordinated.

The Will

The will is the power by which we desire goods known through the intellect. Thus, voluntary acts are those caused by the will, which in Latin is voluntas. An act necessitated by an outside agent is then incompatible with voluntariness. Other forms of necessity, however, are not - for instance, the need to use certain means to achieve an end chosen by the will or the natural tendency inherent in the will to tend to the good. But the will does not will necessarily everything that it wills. This is possible because, although there are certain things like happiness which the will necessarily desires, there are many goods which have no necessary connection with the former, and so the will is not necessitated by them. The intellect understands that many goods are only relatively good, and so the will can take them or leave them.

The question of the relative value and importance of the intellect and will is of some theoretical and practical interest. Inasmuch as the object of the intellect is more simple and absolute, we must say that it is in itself higher than the will. This does not mean, however, that every act of knowing is better than the corresponding act of willing. Here, what is known and willed makes a difference. If it is something lower than the soul, like a beautiful statue, then the knowing of it is better than the loving of it. But if it is something higher, like God, then love is better. We must also inquire how the will interacts with the other powers. The intellect makes the will act by providing it with knowledge of the good to be sought. On the other hand, in seeking such a good, the will acts as an efficient cause of the activity of all the other powers, except the vegetative, which are not subject to it. But it guides all the others, even the intellect, somewhat as a general causes all the movements of his troops.

Freedom

Experience clearly shows that man is free. Otherwise all advice, exhortations, laws, punishments and rewards would make no sense. Thus, men are different from brutes, which may be aware that they are doing something but do not do it freely. For instance, when a lamb sees a wolf, he knows he must flee and he does, without having any alternative in regard to either the knowing or the acting. But when a man acts he is guided by his judgments, which do not result from any instinct which would determine them in any way, but which he forms objectively. Nor is there anything which determines the will to follow one judgment rather than another. On the contrary, the will chooses on its own which judgment to be guided by.

Our Knowledge Of Bodies

We may best approach this problem historically, by seeing what the earliest philosophers thought about it. The first Greek thinkers held that only bodies existed: they had no notion of spiritual beings. Since material things seem to be in constant change, they believed it impossible to have any certitude. Plato, however, in order to show how true and sure knowledge could be had through the intellect, postulated above such material beings another type that was immaterial and unchanging, and which he called species or ideas. The sciences, definitions and all intellectual knowledge were of these immaterial things, not of the physical, which were only copies of the former. Thus we do not know the things of this world but only those of another, higher one. However, Plato was obviously wrong in this matter, since the object of our sciences is patently physical bodies. His error resulted from this, that he thought that the form that is known must exist in the same way in both the subject and the object. As these forms exist in the knowing subject in an immaterial, universal and unchanging way, he believed that they had to exist in the same manner in the object known. This, however, is not at all necessary. Even the forms found in physical objects exist there in different ways. For instance, some things are whiter than others. Similarly, forms may have different modes of existing in objects and in the mind. Thus the intellect in an immaterial and unchanging way possesses forms that are, in objects, material and changing.

The Basis Of Knowledge

Because the early Greeks held that like was known by like, they maintained that since we know bodies the soul had to be itself a body. Being material, however, cannot be what makes us capable of knowing. By matter a form is limited to being an individual entity, whereas the knower takes on a multitude of different forms. What makes knowledge possible then is to be the opposite of matter: immateriality. Thus, beings which, like plants, receive forms only in a material way do not know. And the more immaterially forms are received, the more perfect a kind of knowledge is it. We must likewise reject any theory which would explain knowledge through innate ideas. If we had any, we would necessarily be aware of them. Then too, the falsity of such a view is shown by the fact that if we lack one of the senses, we also lack a whole area of corresponding ideas.

Main Theories Of Knowledge

According to Democritus, only material things exist, and knowledge consists in one object impressing on another material impressions of itself. As a result, there is for him no difference between sense and intellect. Plato, on the other hand, did say they were different and further that the intellect, which is spiritual, does not use a physical organ in knowing. Moreover, since the spiritual cannot be directly affected by a material cause, he held that intellectual knowledge cannot result from the intellect being acted upon by sensible objects, but only from its participation in the self-subsisting intelligible ideas. He likewise conceived of sense knowledge as a purely spiritual activity, saying that the sense organs, which are material, are affected by other material objects and that at this time the senses, which are spiritual, activate themselves to produce sensible species of those objects. Thus, according to Plato, intellectual knowledge is not based on sense knowledge, nor is the latter really an effect of sensible objects. Aristotle, on the other hand, steered a middle course between Democritus and Plato. He admitted the essential difference between sense and intellectual knowledge. Sensing, he said, is not an act of the soul alone, but is the reaction of the composite of body and soul to the object which is acting upon it. The intellect, on the other hand, operates without using a physical organ. Since the material cannot affect the spiritual, sense knowledge of itself cannot cause intellectual knowledge. There have then to be two intellectual powers. The active intellect abstracts from the sense species the intelligible forms, thereby actualizing them, and impresses them onto the passive intellect, which thereupon understands them. Thus sensations are neither the total nor the efficient causes of intellectual knowledge, but are only a sort of material cause. Thomas concludes from this that, in his present state, all of man's thinking is necessarily accompanied by sense images. As a result, although the intellect itself does not use a physical organ, thinking is impeded if our sense organs are damaged, because the senses cannot then provide the images whence the intellect derives its concepts or to which it relates them. The basic reason why man's thinking always involves sense images is that our intellects have as their proper object the quiddity or essence of physical things. Our minds are structured to know them primarily. Consequently, we know spiritual realities only in function of our knowledge of material objects.

Comment

In the thirteenth century the West had translations of only a couple of Plato's works. So, Aquinas had to rely on secondary sources for his knowledge of Plato's views, which fact accounts for the historical inaccuracy of his **exposition** of them. Actually, the theories which Thomas attributes to Plato are a combination of Plato's and Augustine's.

Abstraction

To "abstract" means to consider one thing apart from another. Thus, we can consider the color of an apple without considering the apple itself. We can likewise know what it is, for instance, to be a man while leaving aside all the individuating characteristics of any individual man. This is what is meant by the intellectual abstraction of an essence. This stripping of the individuating conditions from an intelligible form is done by the active intellect, whereas the reception of this abstracted form into itself by the passive intellect constitutes the act of conceiving or understanding. We could put it another way. The form as it exists in the object and in our perception of that object is only potentially intelligible. The active intellect makes it actually intelligible by abstracting it from the perception, and thus material forms exist in an immaterial way in the passive intellect.

The Role Of The Species

Many of the ancient philosophers erred in regard to the role of the forms or species possessed by the knower, insofar as they thought that the subject knows only the received species, not the object itself, that we know, for instance, our sensations but not the sensed object. Such a view, however, makes all knowledge purely subjective. Moreover, it results in doing away with the distinction between truth and falsity by making everything we think true. Actually the species, be it sensible or intelligible, is not what is directly known; it is rather that by which the object is known. We might compare it to a picture, by which we are made to know that an object looks like, but there is this difference that we have to know the picture itself first for it to produce that effect, whereas the cognitive species produces the same kind of effect without our having to be aware of the species. In fact, we usually are not aware of it but realize its presence only when we introspect ourselves. What we do directly know is the object itself, of which the species is a representation of a sort. We must say then that our knowledge is objective, although in varying degrees, and so can be partly or completely true or false. Note also that our knowledge may be incomplete, but this would not make it false, unless we thought we had complete knowledge. But this would be naive, as we have complete knowledge of nothing.

Comment

Although Aquinas was here attacking the relativist and idealist views of some old Greek thinkers, nevertheless his objections are also valid against their modern versions, which have dominated much of European thought in the last three centuries. We are referring to such men as Berkeley, Hume, Kant and Hegel.

Intellectual Knowledge Of Singulars

Because of the way that we know, our intellect does not perceive material objects primarily in their singularity. As we have seen, the intellect knows through abstraction. It grasps the nature of a physical object by leaving aside its individuating conditions. Thus, what it attains primarily is the universal nature of the object. To know intellectually an individual, physical object is possible for us only in a reflex manner, by relating our universal concept of it with our sense perceptions of it.

Man's Knowledge Of Himself

An object is knowable only to the extent that it is actual. But since the intellect is a potency, we cannot then know it in itself, only its operation. Thus, that we have an intellect is easily seen by everyone. However, to know what the intellect is requires diligent and precise study, so that many are in ignorance or in error concerning it. The same would hold about the habits of the intellect.

Knowledge After Death

It might seem impossible for the soul to know after a man's death, because in its present condition the soul cannot know except, as we have seen, by referring its concepts back to its perceptions. Since the soul at death is separated from the body, it can no longer have perceptions, as these require a physical organ. And so, apparently, it could no longer think. We must understand, however, that every being's manner of operating is proportioned to its mode of existence. As a result, the soul's operations when separated are different from when it is united to the body. In the former case the soul will know by basing itself on the previously acquired species it has retained and also on those which it receives, as do the angels, through participation in the divine being. Consequently it will have only a rather general sort of cognition of many things, although it will continue to have an individual knowledge of objects met before death.

Comment

Aquinas discusses at length many other questions about how man acts in Part I-II.

QQ. 103-119: GOD'S GOVERNANCE OF THE WORLD

Does God Govern The World?

Some ancient philosophers, like Democritus and Epicurus, denied that God governed the world, saying that everything happens by chance. But this is impossible. In the first place, we see nature always or generally producing what is more proper. But this would not happen unless it was being, made to tend to some goal. This, however, is precisely what is meant by government. Secondly, since God has created every finite being and it would be contrary to his infinite goodness not to bring them to their natural term of perfection, it follows that he must arrange matters that they will achieve their end. But again this is to govern them.

The Divine Purpose

Everything tends to fulfill its own function in the universe, so we can say that the very order of the universe is what they are made to maintain. But this order cannot be in itself God's ultimate end in governing. Since he existed prior to the world, we must say that he is himself the reason why he both causes and governs the universe. Loving his infinite goodness, he wills to share it with creatures and to establish an order that will ensure their participation in it.

Extension Of Divine Government

Since God is the cause of all things, he also necessarily governs them all, inasmuch as to produce something and to bring it to its perfection pertain to the same agent. The same conclusion follows from the fact that they all have the same end to which he has ordered them. It might be objected, however, that since God made men free they govern themselves, so that God does not govern everything. We must remember, however, that since the universe is made up of different kinds of beings, how they are ruled must vary accordingly. Thus, God could not use moral laws to govern irrational creatures, as he does with intelligent beings.

Effects Of Divine Government

We can, in general, distinguish several such effects. In the first place, creatures are made to participate more fully in God's goodness. Then too, in achieving this, God has to conserve things in existence and also help them to achieve their proper goods. Thus, there are innumerable particular instances of his governing activities manifested. Basically all creatures can be said to be continually maintained in existence by God, inasmuch as they would simply cease being if he for a moment stopped exercising his divine power in maintenance of them. We can show it in this way. Every effect depends on its cause, but in different ways and in accord with the type of causality exercised. Some agents only cause their effects to take such and such a form, but do not cause these effects to exist. When a contractor builds a house he is its cause only in the sense that the coming together of the parts depends on him, but the continuing existence of the house does not depend on him, since the house continues to be after the contractor is dead. Thus, the cause of an effect's becoming and of its being are not always the same. In fact, they are usually different. But just as the becoming of an effect ceases as soon as its cause stops its causal activity, so a being will cease to exist as soon as the cause of its being stops its activity. A cause, however, is such only inasmuch as it is in act. Since God is the pure act of existence, only he can be the ultimate cause of the existence of finite beings, and they continue to exist only as long as he continues to cause them to. We should note, though, that God in maintaining things in existence works through secondary causes usually, and these too are said to conserve an object in existence. Nevertheless, God remains the first and principal cause of all these effects.

Divine Action In The World

God governs the universe not just by keeping it in existence, but also by concurring in all the activities of his creatures. This was denied, for instance, by many Mohammedan theologians. Nevertheless it is true. By "concurrence" we mean that God and creatures acting together cause whatever occurs. Now this happens in various ways. God concurs as telic or final cause because he is the supreme good. But every act seeks to achieve some good, which is such only inasmuch as it is a participation in the divine goodness. Thus God is the telic cause of every act. He concurs as an efficient cause too since, as we saw in the second Way, he is the first efficient cause of every activity. He concurs also as a formal cause, inasmuch as he causes and conserves in existence the quiddity of all the secondary efficient causes he works through.

SUMMA THEOLOGICA

TEXTUAL ANALYSIS

PART I-II

INTRODUCTION

Contents

Having discussed God and his creatures, Thomas now turns his attention to problems of general moral theory: man, since he has an intellect and free will, is responsible for his actions and is thus rather similar to God; but what are the basic considerations by which he must guide himself? The main points Thomas takes up in this section are: man's end, human acts, morality, the passions, habits, virtue, sin, law and grace. This last, however, pertains to theology.

Significance

This part of the *Summa* remains one of the great classics in the literature of ethics. It has served as the basis of numerous later works, and as a result its originality is nowadays hard to appreciate, as we have become so familiar with its main ideas. At the time of its composition, however, the work was revolutionary. Although there was perhaps not one completely new idea or theory in it, many of the views it propounded were generally unaccepted at the time or represented novel interpretations of accepted notions. The logicality of the arrangement, the comprehensiveness of the materials and the unity, strength and consistency of the treatment also marked a new stage in the development of moral theorizing. Its unity does not preclude it from being nevertheless a synthesis of elements taken from the moralists of the preceding millennium and a half. Nor does the consistency of the basic doctrines extend to the working out of details: Thomas wrote so fast he necessarily left loose ends on occasion.

QQ. 1-5: MAN'S END

Human Acts And Ends

We must distinguish between acts of man and human acts. When a person acts freely and with knowledge of what he is doing, he is responsible for it, and it is only this kind of action that can be properly called a human act. All others we may designate as acts of man. Human acts then are caused by a man through his intellect and will. The object of the will, however, is a good considered as an end. Thus every human act is done for an end, which is freely sought. However, at any point in our life we are seeking many ends simultaneously. These we seek because of their interrelations: some are wanted in order to get others, and there is one to which all the others are subordinated. This we call the ultimate end. It is impossible for us to desire simultaneously diverse goods as ultimate ends.

For, as every being naturally tends to its own perfection, we desire only that as our ultimate end which we consider our perfect and complete good. Whatever good we desire, realizing that it is not perfect, we can tend to only insofar as it is a means to get our perfect good. Everybody agrees as to what in the abstract is our ultimate end: the perfect good. But there is little agreement as to what concretely this would consist in. Thus some would say it is riches; others, pleasure, and so forth. But there is necessarily one supreme good only which could objectively serve as the ultimate end for all men. This we call beatitude or happiness, and it consists in the knowledge and love of God.

Beatitude

By "end" we can mean two different things. We may mean the object itself that we desire, as money is the end of misers. Or, we may mean the possession or enjoyment of that object. Taking it in the first way, only God because of his infinite goodness could be our ultimate end. Taking it in the second way, we call the possession or enjoyment of God beatitude. But since man's ultimate end is also, as we have seen, the perfecting of himself, beatitude consists of an operation of man, because activity is the ultimate perfection of every agent. It obviously could not be an operation of the senses, because we do not attain to God through them. It is impossible too that it consist in the acts of the will, which are to desire and enjoy. For when we desire an end, we do not have it yet; and when we enjoy it, it is because we have previously attained it. Beatitude is to be found essentially then in the operation of the intellect, although the will with its delight over the possessed good provides the consummation of our beatitude. We may further distinguish between an imperfect and a perfect beatitude. The former would consist of the knowledge we have of the things of this world. This provides a certain satisfaction, but it clearly cannot be man's ultimate end. Our ultimate and perfect beatitude can consist only in a vision of the divine essence. For we know from his effects that God exists but, not knowing him as he is in himself, we cannot rest until we achieve such knowledge. Perfect beatitude will require then that the intellect arrive at a knowledge of the very essence of the first cause. To achieve the imperfect beatitude we are capable of in this life, we obviously need the body, health, strength, a minimum of physical goods and friends. None of these, however, is necessary to achieve perfect beatitude. Thus, as regards the body, the intellect needs it only to provide the sensory basis from which it draws its concepts. But as God is not attained by the senses in any way, the intellect will not achieve its knowledge of God through them, and so the soul can attain blessedness without the body.

The Attainment Of Beatitude

That we are capable of this is clear from the fact that through our intellect we can know the universal and perfect good and through our will desire it. Since some men, however, are better developed and disposed than others, they can possess their ultimate end in a fuller and higher manner. Unlike the imperfect happiness we attain in this life and which is often lost because of a variety of causes, the perfect beatitude of the future life cannot be lost, because we would never cease to want it since it consists of our supreme good, and God could never make us cease to have it, as this would entail an injustice on his part. To attain it, however, it is necessary that we prepare ourselves for it, and this we do by our various acts.

QQ. 6-17: HUMAN ACTS

Voluntariness

Since beatitude is the proper good of man, we acquire it primarily through those acts that are properly human. These then we may now consider in some detail as regards their general characteristics. One of these is voluntariness. To be voluntary an act must proceed from an inner principle, but this in itself does not make it voluntary. For in brutes the sense appetites are inner principles whence proceed actions, but these obviously are not what we mean by voluntary acts. The basic reason is that the brutes act blindly without knowing as such the end for which they act. Men, however, can know as such the end to which they are tending. So we call an action voluntary when both the act and its directedness to a known end proceed from an inner principle. The latter is the power, capacity or faculty that we call the rational appetite or will Thus the more perfectly a person is aware of the consequences of his acts and wants to continue them, the more voluntary they are. It is not merely positive actions that are voluntary. Willing not to do an act involves voluntariness just as much as willing to do it.

Modifiers Of Voluntariness

We must distinguish two types of voluntary actions. There is one which flows immediately from the will: the very act of willing. The other consists of the actions ordered by the will and performed by other powers, for instance, to walk. The latter can be contravened through violence; the former cannot. By violence we mean the application of an outside force to make us do something. If, then, we are made to do something through violence, this is contrary to our will and involuntary on our part. The situation is, however, rather different in those cases in which something is done out of fear. Here there is a certain amount of voluntariness and also of involuntariness, but more of the former. Acts done out of fear, we may say, are basically voluntary while being involuntary in this way: that we would prefer to be in a situation such that we could act differently. Take, for example, the captain of a heavily loaded ship at sea in a storm. To avoid sinking, he may choose to jettison the cargo. This is in and by itself voluntary, but had there been no storm he would not have made such a choice. He would, moreover, have preferred not to make it, so in that restricted sense we can say the act is involuntary. We must then be careful to distinguish those actions caused by violence and those which arise from fear of violence.

The passions are another factor we must consider. Rather than making actions less voluntary, they usually have the effect of making them more so. For by voluntary we mean that which the will desires. However, the will is inclined through the passions to desire that which excited them, and thus the passions can increase voluntariness. In those cases, however, where passion is such that it makes deliberation completely impossible, obviously the resulting actions are not voluntary. Another modifier of voluntariness is ignorance, which makes actions involuntary to the extent that it prevents one from having the knowledge required for voluntariness. It is clear, however, that ignorance does not always cause involuntariness, as in those cases when we would do the same action even if we had the requisite knowledge, or when the ignorance itself is wanted as an excuse for doing the act, or when the ignorance concerns matters about which we can and should be informed.

Circumstances Surrounding Moral Acts

Whenever we perform a human act, we do it under a set of conditions which are themselves different from the act, but which affect it in one way or another. These we call the circumstances. Speaking analogically, we can say that the circumstances are the accidents of the act. The circumstances, though accidents, are important from a moral point of view. An act can serve as a means to the ultimate end only if it has the proper circumstances. Then too, an act is more or less good or bad depending on the circumstances. Following Aristotle, we may recognize eight main types of circumstances: who does the act? what does he do? by what means? where? why? in what manner? when? to what? Of all of these, the purpose of the act, or why it is done, is the most important, because the end is the object of the will, and the act is a human one to the extent that it is voluntary. The second in importance is what is done. The importance of the others will vary according to how they happen to affect the act.

Comment

It seems rather peculiar to speak of what is done and the end of the act as accidental to the act. It would be better to speak of these as constituting the substance of the act, and the other circumstances as being its accidents.

The Object Of The Will

The will is our spiritual appetite, as contrasted with our sensory appetites. Only the good, however, can be the object of an appetite. For an appetite is that whereby we tend to something, but nothing tends to something else except to the extent that the latter is suitable for it. This suitability is found in some form in every being and is what we call its goodness. However, unlike the natural inclinations found in plants and inaninate objects, the appetites, be they sensory or rational, tend only to known goods. Thus, what the will tends to does not have to actually be a good for it, but it must be perceived by the person as a good, otherwise it would not be desired. When a person tends to a good, it thereby becomes for him an end. Properly speaking, the object of the will is its ends, for the means to an end are willed not for themselves, but only inasmuch as they are ordered to an end. Thus, sometimes, we might will an end without the means thereto or both an end and its means, but we could never will the means without at the same time willing the corresponding end.

What Moves The Will?

In one way the will moves itself; in other ways it is moved by other causes. The intellect moves the will by presenting to it a good which it may tend to. The sense appetites can move the will by inclining us to see objects in a light other than what we otherwise would. However, the will is able to move itself to want the means for the ends it desires. It also moves itself insofar as it can make the intellect think of one good or another which it can then tend to as an end. But God also moves the will insofar as he gives the will its natural inclination to tend to the good.

How The Will Is Moved

There are some things which the will by its very nature has to tend to; for instance, the good in general, beatitude, the satisfaction of the other human powers, and life itself. In regard to whether the will is moved necessarily by anything we must distinguish. The will can be moved in two ways: simply to act or to act in a certain way. In regard to the first, the simple exercise of the will, nothing can necessitate it, because we can always refuse to think of a certain object and then we will never desire it. In regard to the second, the specification of the willed act, sometimes the object necessitates the will and sometimes not. If something would seem to be an absolute good, we could not help but want it. In point of fact, however, we usually in this life find the goods we encounter to be deficient in some way or another and so are not necessitated by them. An objection here might be raised as to whether the sense appetites might not necessitate the will. They cannot, however. Now in some cases the passions are so strong that they completely becloud the mind and make us act in a certain way. But here there is no act of the will. In those cases when the passions allow us to judge to some extent they cannot necessitate the will.

Comment

Thomas' psychology here seems rather questionable. We do not think that even the most vehement passions ever prevent the intellect and will from working, so that the will can be necessitated by a passion, inasmuch as it can make a particular good seem so desirable that we have to desire it.

QQ. 18-21: MORALITY

Good And Evil

Just as things are good to the extent that they have their due plenitude of being and evil to the degree that they lack it, so also are all actions either good or evil for the same reason. But the due plenitude of being of anything is determined by that which gives it its quiddity. Thus the goodness of an act derives from four sources: from the mere fact of being, from its object, from its circumstances and from its end. Of these, the end is the most important in regard to an act being good or bad, then the object, then the circumstances. Whatever is in accord with the objectively rational order of ends is good; whatever is not, is bad. Hence if we consider acts in a generic manner and apart from their circumstances, some, like giving alms, are by their nature good and others, like stealing, are essentially wrong. Some, however, like moving a rock, are indifferent, since in themselves they neither implement nor disturb the moral order. But no act is indifferent when we consider it as actually performed and with all of its circumstances. For whatever is done is done for some purpose, which will have to be either in accord with or contrary to the order of reason, when all the circumstances are considered. Basically, morality is determined by the end and the object of an act, but in some cases what is usually merely a circumstance may be so closely related to the object of the act as to have to be considered a part of it, and so may change the moral nature of the act. For instance, where an evil act is done is usually not of great importance morally. If, however, the act is stealing and it is done in the church treasury, this makes it a sacrilege. Circumstances do not always change the moral species of the act, but usually just make it less good or bad. Thus, although a theft of five thousand dollars is worse than one of four thousand, they both belong to the same moral category.

Morality Of The Interior Acts Of The Will

The goodness or evil of these acts depend, of course, on the object willed, but since we can desire this object only according to the manner in which it is known through the intellect, morality also depends on our understanding. However, although human reason is thus the rule and measure of morality, it is such only because it reflects what is ordered by the divine plan for the universe. Hence the goodness of a man's will depends more on the divine eternal law than upon his own reason. But here another problem arises. Does a man do wrong if he does not follow an erroneous conscience? Or, to put it in another way, are we morally obliged to follow any mistaken judgment that we make? We must answer that whoever wills to do what he thinks is evil is guilty whether or not he was correct in his evaluation of the act. But can we say that a man who follows an erroneous conscience does good? As long as the error is not deliberate or about what we should be informed about, such an act does not entail guilt.

Comment

Thomas does not seem to draw here the full conclusions which flow from his premises. If our conscience is the measure and rule of our acts, whatever we do in good faith has to be at least subjectively good, even if it is objectively a violation of the moral order.

Consequences Of Good And Bad Acts

Inasmuch as our human acts are those over which we have control, their goodness and badness are imputed to us: we are held responsible for them. Consequently it is only such voluntary actions that make us subject to praise or to blame. It is only such too than can cause us merit or demerit. Whenever we do something which is to the advantage or disadvantage of someone else, there is a need in justice for a corresponding retribution, for rewards or punishments. This is what we call a merit or demerit. We may have them in reference either to single persons or to groups.

QQ. 22-48: THE PASSIONS

The Passions

In general, the reception of anything is referred to as a passion. Thus, even sensation and intellection are partially passive, processes. More properly, however, the word refers, when speaking of man, to the movements of the sense appetites, which are so strongly affected and attracted by their objects. There are two sense appetites. The concupiscible appetite is the power by which we tend to the simply pleasurable sensory good and away from its contrary. Sometimes, however, we have struggles or difficulties to achieve this good or to flee its contrary evil. The appetite by which we react to such difficulties we call the irascible. There are two corresponding genera of passions and several species of passions of each. Thus the concupiscible passions are joy, sadness, desire, aversion, love and hate. The irascible are hope, despair, fear, daring and anger. In themselves the passions are neither good nor bad, since they are of the sense appetites and so do not derive from reason. They have moral value, however, insofar as they are subject to the reason and will. The ancient Stoics held that all passions were evil; because they did not distinguish between the sensory and intellectual levels, they conceived of the passions as appetitive processes which went beyond the limits of reason and were hence evil. The Peripatetics, the followers of Aristotle, were correct in rejecting such a view and holding that passions are morally good when held within the bounds of moderation, and that they are in this way great aids in achieving moral perfection.

Love

The term love can be used in relation to any tendency, be it purely physical, sensory or intellectual. It is thus an analogical term, and we must be careful in every case to understand in precisely what sense it is being used. When taken to mean a movement of a sense appetite, it is a passion of the concupiscible and is primary within that genus. For sadness, aversion and hate, being concerned with the painful evil, derive from the passions concerned with the corresponding goods. But among these, love necessarily precedes desire and joy.

Pleasure

Whenever anything acts according to its nature, it achieves a certain perfection. If it is an animal it can be aware of the situation, that it has attained to a good, to which it may react through the sense or rational appetites. This reaction is what we call pleasure. Thus it is sometimes a passion of the sense appetite, but sometimes something higher, a movement of the will. It is obvious that intellectual pleasures are more perfect and desirable than those of the senses, but the latter can nevertheless be more vehement. Pleasure causes in us a kind of expansion, insofar as we become aware that we have achieved a certain good and, so to speak, enfold and rest in it. Pleasure sometimes helps us to operate more efficiently, but physical pleasures may impede the work of the intellect. This can happen in different ways, by distracting our attention or by attaching us to other objects. Some philosophers of antiquity held that all pleasures were evil, but in this they erred, for pleasure is merely the satisfaction of an appetite in some operation or end. But goodness and evil refer to whether or not something is in accord with the objectively rational order of things. Thus any pleasure resulting from that which is good will be itself good, while the pleasures which derive from bad actions are evil. We must then also reject the view of the Epicureans, who held that all pleasures were good and who indeed made pleasure the measure of good and evil. Now in regard to the latter they were not completely wrong, for we can distinguish between good and bad men on the basis of what they find their greatest pleasure in, but we can do this only because we know on other grounds which pleasures are good and which are evil.

QQ. 49-54: HABITS

Nature Of Habits

After having taken up human acts and the various passions which may affect them, Thomas now turns to their intrinsic principles. These are our powers and habits. The former were considered in Part I. So there remain the habits. A habit is defined by Aristotle as any kind of disposition which is hard to change. It belongs therefore to the category of quality, of which it is only one of several species. Thus, health is a habit, because by it we are disposed to function in a physiologically normal manner. Habits are necessary since they are perfections of their possessor. When a power is determined by its very nature to act only in one given way, then it needs no habits. But when it is capable of a diversity of operations, habits are necessary to establish a given pattern of activity. Thus, the power of seeing has no habits, but the imagination does.

Where Are Habits Found?

Since a habit is a disposition of some subject that is in potency either to some form or to some operation, the body then, as opposed to the soul, can be said to have habits, such as health or beauty. It cannot, however, be the principal subject of operational habits, since all the actions which flow directly from it are all completely without variation. The soul, however, is through its various powers the subject of numerous habits. Properly speaking, the souls of brutes can have no operational habits, since whatever they do is determined according to instinctive or conditioned patterns. In man, however, whatever sensory powers can under the direction of reason vary their operations are foci of habits. It is clear then that the passive intellect has many habits; for instance, wisdom and the various sciences. Likewise the will too has many; for instance, the habit of acting with kindness or justice.

Growth And Loss Of Habits

Entitative habits, like health, may be given us totally by nature or may result partly from nature and partly from an exterior principle; e.g., a doctor. On the other hand, operational habits never result totally from nature. Usually these are the effect of multiple actions of the same type. For instance, a pitcher can develop control only through practice. In some cases, however, a habit can be established by one action. The intensity of habits may be increased by performance of actions in accordance with them. A few habits, like that of the first theoretical principles, cannot be lost. Most of them can, however, through the acquisition of their contraries. They can also be lost or diminished by not using them.

The Varieties Of Habits

It is clear enough that the same power can have several habits. But how are we to distinguish one habit from another? Since habits are dispositions to act, they will differ in their species on the same basis as actions, which are categorized according to their objects. Thus, truthfulness and justice are two different virtues, because one is concerned with the quality of our speech, and the other with the quality of our interpersonal relations. A specific difference between habits may also arise on the basis of its relation to the order of nature. If a habit disposes us to act according to the requirements of our nature, it is good; otherwise, it is evil.

QQ. 55-67: VIRTUE

The Nature Of Virtue

How a person acts depends on his character, because activity always reflects what kind of being the agent is. Now, men are born with certain capabilities which are not determined to a given pattern of expression. These have then to be provided by habits. When these habits are good, that is, when they effect actions which bring us in an orderly and efficient way closer to our ultimate end, we call them virtues. They are found in the intellect, will and sense appetites.

Intellectual Virtues

A habit may be a virtue in two ways: it may make us capable of acting well or it may cause us to act well. The habits of the speculative intellect can be said to be virtues only in the first way. Thus, by having the science of grammar, which is an intellectual virtue, we are enabled to speak correctly, but are not made to do so regularly. Since the function of the speculative intellect is the contemplation of truth, which we can do in three ways, it can be perfected by the virtues of understanding, wisdom and the various sciences. Understanding is the habitual cognition of the self-evident principles of being and thinking. Wisdom is the habitual cognition of the ultimate causes of all things, whereby we can judge of all things in proper perspective. The sciences are the habitual cognition of demonstrated conclusions about a certain type of object. The practical intellect has various virtues also: the arts and prudence. Art is the habitual cognition of how to do something correctly. Prudence is the habit by which we judge rightly about how we should act.

Comment

One might question the validity of the initial distinction Thomas makes here. On empirical grounds, it seems rather doubtful that there is any habit which does not also incline us more or less strongly to act in a certain manner. Thus, in order to commit a solecism, a skilled grammarian would usually have to make a deliberate effort to go contrary to his usual manner of speaking.

The Difference Between Intellectual And Moral Virtues

It might seem that all virtues are moral virtues. But this is not so. If you are asked whether someone is moral, you would not be answering the question if you said he was intelligent. A consideration of the etymology of the word "moral" shows why. It comes from mos, which means either a custom or a national inclination to act in a certain way. Since actions result from the appetites, only their virtues then are to be called moral. Moral virtues can be possessed without having such intellectual virtues as wisdom, the sciences and the arts, but not without understanding and prudence. On the other hand, except for prudence, all the intellectual virtues can be found in people who lack the moral virtues.

Comment

The etymological argument used here seems fallacious, because irrelevant. When we speak of moral virtues we are not using "moral" in its etymological sense. Another inconsistency: how could one have the virtue of prudence unless he also to some degree has wisdom?

Cardinal Virtues

When we refer without any qualifications to virtue, we mean human virtues. But to be perfect, human virtue must not only make us capable of acting well but must also cause us to act well. Since the perfect are obviously of greater import than the imperfect, the moral virtues, which include the rectitude of the appetites, must be considered as superior to the intellectual. We must make an exception of prudence, which, although it is an intellectual virtue basically, is by its subject matter a moral virtue too. There are four cardinal virtues, inasmuch as the moral life requires the perfection of four powers and four corresponding areas of activity. Man's intellect is perfected morally by prudence; the will, by justice, the virtue by which we render to every man his due; the concupiscible appetite, by temperance; and the irascible appetite, by fortitude. These four virtues can by themselves establish a rational order in at least most of our activities and so they are the only cardinal virtues.

Virtue As A Mean

To say that virtue consists in following a happy medium in all things might seem to condemn men to a deadening mediocrity. But, as Aristotle indicated, the contrary is true. Moral virtues perfect our activity. But our activity is the more perfect the more closely it conforms to the requirements of our reason. If it exceeds or does not reach these requirements, it misses its mark. Hence virtue is found in the middle ground between excess and deficiency, in reference to the measure of reason. It is then the mean relative to us, not merely a mathematical one. We may note, however, that in the case of justice the mean to be followed is both mathematical and relative. Thus, if you owe someone six dollars, justice requires that you pay exactly that. However, if you have to reduce, the amount of food you should take depends on your physical condition, and this amount would vary from one person to another. Hence, virtue does not entail mediocrity, because the mean between the excess and defect of what ought to be done may, from another point of view, be an extreme. Thus, the religious who take the vow of poverty are going to the limit as far as ownership is concerned, but are following the mean between having superfluous property and being in starving penury.

Relative Value Of The Virtues

Because it is more universal, the object of the intellect, which is truth, is more noble than the object of the will, which is the good. If, then, we consider the virtues absolutely, the intellectual virtues are likewise more noble than the moral. If, however, we consider the virtues relative to activity, the moral fulfill more perfectly the notion of virtue since they incline us to act. They also are more necessary for life. But even this indicates the superiority of the intellectual, which are not thus merely useful but are desired for themselves. Among the moral, justice is the most excellent not only because it perfects the will, which is more similar to the intellect than are the other appetites, but also because it deals with something more important, our relations with our fellow men. Fortitude is the next most valuable because it is concerned with establishing rational order in what we do when sometimes our very lives may depend on it. Then comes temperance, which establishes order in our day to day life. It is obvious that among the intellectual virtues wisdom is the greatest, since it knows and orders all things.

QQ. 71-89: SIN AND VICE

The Nature Of Sin And Vice

A sin is a bad human act. Acts, however, are bad insofar as they do not measure up to the proper rule of the will. There are two such rules: one is our reason; the other is God's, which is basic. We can then accept Augustine's definition of sin as any work, deed or desire against God's eternal law. A vice, on the other hand, is a habit of doing bad acts. Vice then is the contrary of virtue. A man cannot simultaneously have a virtue and its corresponding vice, even though he may have a virtue and perform a sin which is opposed to it. It was an error of both the Stoics and of certain heretics that all sins are equal. Obviously, however, some sins involve a greater disturbance of the moral order than others and so are worse. Thus the sins of the spirit are worse than those of the flesh. This clearly is to be taken only in a general sense: it does not mean that every spiritual fault is worse than any sin of the flesh. The gravity of a sin also depends on how voluntary it is. It can, moreover, be increased by the circumstances.

Sin And The Passions

Socrates, the teacher of Plato, thought that knowledge could never be overcome by the passions. He consequently held that all virtue was knowledge, and all sin, ignorance. In this he was only partially right. He would say that since the will tends only to the good or to the apparent good, it would never tend to anything that is evil except through ignorance or error. We must, however, distinguish. To act rightly, we must be guided by knowledge both of principles and of how they apply in our particular case. We may, however, have full knowledge but be prevented by our passions from using that knowledge. Thus, sin is not synonymous with ignorance. Hence, too, are such sins rightly described as resulting from our weakness. We can thereby also understand why an inordinate love of self is the cause of all sin. But does passion then make it impossible to sin? We must again distinguish, between antecedent and consequent passion. Sin consists essentially in a free choice of the will to do wrong. If passion arises antecedently to the act of the will to do something, it may affect our intellect and will to a greater or lesser degree, even to the extent of making a sin impossible. Consequent passion, on the other hand, does not diminish sin, but rather increases it, or at least is a sign of the will's desire to sin.

The Stain Of Sin

The word "stain" refers properly to physical things like clothes which get dirty and lose their attractiveness. We may, however, metaphorically speak of sin as staining the soul, because when we sin we violate the twofold source of the splendor of the soul, our reason and the divine law. This stain remains even after the sin itself, but it can be erased by a contrary movement of the will, whereby we return to our previous position in regard to our end.

QQ. 90-108: LAW

The Nature Of Law

We must now consider the factors exterior to us which affect our acts. Among them are the laws. First of all, we might ask whether laws pertain primarily to the intellect, will or some other faculty. Since we mean by law a certain rule and measure of action, by which we are led to act or not to act, and since the rule and measure of human acts is the reason, the laws then pertain primarily to the reason. The laws pertain to the will and the other powers, but only insofar as they are to be guided by the intellect. Now, in guiding the intellect, the law must order all things in the light of man's ultimate end, which is happiness. But since man as a social being can achieve happiness only is communion with his fellow men, all law must be ordered to attaining the happiness of all men, that is, the common good. Thus, only the members of the community as a group, or the person in charge of the community who acts in their name, can make laws. It is obvious, however, that if laws are to regulate the actions of men, they have to be made known to them, that is, they have to be promulgated. With this, then, we can define law as an ordinance established for the common good by the one in charge of the community, and promulgated by him.

Types Of Law

Law being what it is, and the universe being ruled by divine providence, the rational principles according to which God runs things are laws. Since God is not in time but eternity, we call them the eternal law. The eternal law is in God as the ruler of the universe, but it is in creatures insofar as they have in themselves inclinations to their proper acts and ends. Rational creatures, however, are guided by divine providence in a much higher way, inasmuch as they participate in it by directing themselves and other things to their ends. This participation in the eternal law by men is called their natural law. It is the impression of the light of the divine truth in us whereby we can then, with the resulting natural light of reason, discern what is right and what is wrong. However, the precepts of the natural law, although universal, are also rather general, so much so that by themselves they are inadequate to guide the actions of men in all necessary ways. We must therefore, after taking into consideration the particular conditions under which we happen to live, extend and complete the natural law with a complementary set of laws, which are our civil laws.

The Eternal Law

The eternal law, we may say, is nothing but the plan of the divine wisdom according to which it directs every being and act. As a result, we all know it, not indeed as it is in God, but inasmuch as we feel its effects. Actually, the knowledge of any truth is a participation in the eternal law, and so we all know it so some degree. All men know the general principles of the natural law, but their knowledge of the rest of it varies. We have seen that any real human law is an extension of the natural law, but as this is a participation in the eternal law, we must also say that all valid laws are derived from the eternal law. We must further say that whatever occurs in creatures, be it necessary or contingent, is subject to the eternal law. Those things, however, which pertain to the divine essence and operations are not subject to the eternal law, but rather are in reality the eternal law itself.

The Natural Law

Just as the speculative intellect knows intuitively the first principles of being and of thinking that govern all things, so also the practical intellect has a direct, immediate grasp of the basic precepts of the natural law, because both types of principles are self-evident. Since the good is that which the practical intellect knows the first and to which it orders all activity, the good is the fundamental notion of the first principle of the practical reason. We may formulate this principle in this way: "Do good and avoid evil." All other precepts of the natural law are derived from this one, since our reason necessarily concludes that whatever it naturally perceives as a human good we must tend to, and that we must avoid the contrary. We perceive something as good, however, insofar as we have a natural inclination to it. Thus we formulate the natural law on the basis of our natural inclinations. First of all, there is the inclination we have in common with all substances - to conserve ourselves. Here the natural law ordains that we do whatever is necessary to maintain life and avoid whatever would harm it. Secondly, there is the inclination to those things that belong to man's animal nature, whence we have the natural law about marriage and the rearing of children. In the third place, there is the inclination to the goods proper to our rational nature, such as the knowledge of truth or life in society. Corresponding to this are the precepts requiring us to avoid undue ignorance and lack of charity.

Universality Of The Natural Law

Besides applying to all men, the natural law can be said to be universal in the sense that it is known by all men, although not in all the same way. In its primary principles it is known, and equally well, by all normal adults. In regard to certain of the precepts derived as conclusions from these primary principles, these are valid for the majority of cases and are known as such by all men. In a few cases, however, these secondary precepts do not apply because of the unusual circumstances involved, and they may not be too well known because of either passion of evil customs. Thus, among the Germans theft was not thought to be evil. The basic reason for the universality of the natural law is that all men have the same nature and ends, despite their often striking accidental differences. They must therefore, in general, attain their ultimate end by activities that are basically the same for all. The variety of activity possible increases, however, the further from the primary principles are the conclusions drawn from these, because of the increasing number of factors which have to be considered and which often cancel each other out.

Immutability Of The Natural Law

Like any other law, the natural law can change by being added to. A change by subtraction, however, is another matter. The natural law cannot change in this manner in its first principles, but it may in its secondary precepts. This occurs only in a few specialized cases when conditions would make the observance of such precepts unreasonable. Similarly then, the broader precepts of the natural law could never cease to be known by men, but some of the others may because of depraved customs or bad upbringing.

Civil Laws

Men have to establish civil laws and punishments for their infraction, because by itself the natural law is insufficient to keep in check those who are prone to vice. These, however, through fear or punishment can usually be prevented from breaking the laws, and, gradually, as the habit of doing what the law ordains becomes stronger in them, they become themselves virtuous. We should note that civil laws can be related to the natural in two ways. They may simply repeat one or another of the natural laws or they may be specifications of them. An example of the first is the law prohibiting murder. An example of the second would be a law positing hanging as the punishment for murder. Since it is the purpose of the laws to direct men in such a manner as to help them achieve their common good, they must be framed accordingly. This means that they must be couched in general terms, so as to hold for the majority of men and cases, and not need to be changed frequently. Then too, although the purpose of the laws is to help make men as virtuous as possible, given the actual imperfection of the majority of them, the laws cannot require them to practice every virtue. On the contrary, they can prohibit only the more serious deficiencies, and especially those that harm others, and the prevention of which is necessary to maintain society. To try to do anything more would only cause disorder. The laws can improve men's characters only gradually, and so the legislators must move slowly and only make laws which they have good reasons to believe will be able to work. It is clear that citizens have a moral obligation to obey all just laws, even when they are onerous. But they would not be obliged to obey any unjust law, except perchance to avoid giving scandal or to avoid causing a turmoil that would serve no purpose. A law, however, could be unjust for various reasons: if the legislator requires services which satisfy more his cupidity or glory than the common good; if the lawmakers go beyond their authority; if they are unfair in their allocation of the burdens of citizenship; and finally, if they pass laws which are contrary to the natural law. In this latter case, no one should obey them.

SUMMA THEOLOGICA

TEXTUAL ANALYSIS

PART II-III

Contents

Having discussed in general terms the moral act, its characteristics and manifestations, Thomas now turns to a detailed consideration of individual virtues and their corresponding vices. First he takes up the "theological" virtues of faith, hope and charity and their opposite vices. These virtues he conceives of as habits infused in us by God, so that the consideration of them does not pertain to philosophy; but since much of what he has to say about them, especially charity, would also be true of the analogous natural virtues and since too his views on them are important for an understanding of his conception of the moral life, we shall treat of them briefly. Thomas then takes up the four cardinal virtues, prudence, justice, fortitude and temperance. He concludes with a discussion of alternative modes of life.

Significance

This part of the *Summa* is by far the longest. The basic approach is one that was used by Plato and Aristotle and was common also among the Christian theologians: to delineate the moral ideal by describing and interrelating all the virtues which a good man should have. Contrast this with the approach usually followed now of discussing morality in terms of the rights and duties that we have. The salient features of Thomas here are the organization of the material under two sets of virtues, the theological and the cardinal, and his highly detailed discussions of the individual virtues and vices, which may seem commonplace to us nowadays, because they have been repeated so often since, but which were at the time often highly original.

QQ. 1-16: FAITH

Faith And Those Who Lack It

Faith is a habit infused by God by which we assent to what he has revealed, simply because he has revealed it. It may follow an investigation of the grounds on which the revelation is accepted, but does not involve any attempt to prove what is revealed. If a person lacks faith just because he has, through no fault of his own, never been able to acquire it, then his infidelity is not a sin. However, anyone who is an infidel out of pride, because he refuses to submit to divine revelation, commits a most serious evil. What then should be done with infidels? The first type should not be compelled to accept the faith, for faith is by its nature a free assent. Those, however, who once accepted the faith should be compelled to keep it as they had promised to.

> **Comment**

Aquinas is inconsistent here. On the basis of his own principles, all infidels should be viewed in the same manner as the first type. The inconsistency, such as it is, results from his inability to conceive of anybody being an honest heretic or apostate.

QQ. 23-46: CHARITY

Nature Of Charity

Charity is a kind of habitual love. But there are different sorts of love. To love something for the good which it procures ourselves is a love of desire, as opposed to a love of friendship, in which we love an object by wanting it to achieve its own good. But to be friendship, such as benevolence must also be mutual. This in turn requires a basis of intercommunication. In the case of charity, it is provided by the beatitude God wishes to share with us. Thus, charity is a friendship between men and God. Of all the virtues it is the most excellent, because through it we came closest to God, our ultimate end. It follows too that it is the foundation and form of every other real virtue. It is then of the essence of charity that we so love God that we desire to submit ourselves in all things to him and to follow all his percepts. Charity will therefore be lost when we commit any act directly contrary to it. This occurs when we deliberately prefer to violate God's precepts rather than keep his friendship, and this is just what we mean by a mortal sin.

The Object Of Charity

The principal object of charity is obviously God himself, but it would also extend to whatever we love because of him. But since we should want our fellow men to attain to God, our charity thus includes them too. Since, however, friendship can exist only between intelligent beings, charity in the proper sense could not extend to subhuman creatures. But must we also love sinners and our enemies? Certainly, but not inasmuch as they are sinners or enemies, but inasmuch as they are persons and thus made in the image of God. In other words, we must hate their sins but love them. It is also necessary that this love of neighbor not remain merely verbal but manifest itself in action to some extent at least, for instance, in rendering aid when it is required.

In What Order Should We Love?

Clearly, some persons should be loved more than others. God should be loved the most, since it is in him that' we shall find our beatitude, whereas we love our neighbor because he participates with us in beatitude. Although one should love God more than oneself, one must love himself more than he does his neighbor; because we love ourselves inasmuch as we participate in God whereas we love our neighbor only inasmuch as he is associated with us in this participation. For similar reasons we should love more those who have closer relationships with us. Thus we should especially love our blood relations. Other things being equal, we should love our fathers more than our mothers because the former are active, but the latter are only passive, principles. Since our parents did give us existence, from this point of view they are for us a greater good than our wives and so should be loved more. Looking at the closeness of the relation between man and wife, on this basis a wife should be loved more than one's parents. We might say then that a more intense love is to be rendered a wife, but greater reverence to parents.

The Manifestations Of Charity

Charity has various effects. It leads us to acts of benevolence, of wanting for others what is good for them. Beyond this, however, it brings about between persons a union that is both spiritual and affective. It thus results further in joy, peace, sympathy, beneficence, the giving of help, both material and spiritual, and the fraternal correction of those at fault. It also represses various vices which are opposed to it: gloominess, which, when carried far enough, can involve dissatisfaction with the highest goods; envy, by which we are saddened by the good which another achieves, because we consider it a diminution of our own glory or worth; pride and vainglory, which lead us to cause all sorts of discord and contention. Charity also prevents schisms, the breaking up of the unity of the faithful; unjust wars, that is, wars which do not fulfill the proper conditions: that they be declared by proper authorities, that they be for a just cause and that they be waged with good motives; feuds, which are a kind of private, and therefore unjust, war; sedition, by which the unity of the state is attacked; and scandal, which is any word or deed which provides to others an occasion for sin. We may note that giving scandal is not always a sin, because some people are scandalized when they ought not to be. A good example of this in our own day are the Southern segregationists who are appalled by those who uphold the civil rights of Negroes.

QQ 47-56: PRUDENCE

Nature Of Prudence

Because a prudent person is one who can choose wisely, prudence might be thought to be a virtue of the will, but this is incorrect. A man is called prudent primarily because he can determine what would be a good solution to a problem, and so prudence is a virtue of the intellect. We may define it as a virtue of the practical intellect by which we are enabled to judge rightly what in concrete cases would be effective and morally proper. It is not then the function of prudence to determine the ends for which we should act, but only to decide what in particular cases are the best means to achieve these ends. It is prudence that discovers in every moral problem what is the virtuous and happy mean to follow. This involves the discovery of different possibilities of action, the judging of their relative value and the commanding of what should be done in the light of both one's own and the common good. True prudence must not be confused with its counterfeit, which we may call cleverness, which is only a degenerate form of prudence and which consists in the ability to work out effective ways of committing evil. Being prudent involves having a number of qualities: a good memory, a grasp of the first principles, docility, ingenuity, practicality, foresight, circumspection and caution.

Vices Opposed To Prudence

These are in general called imprudence. They have various specific forms. Precipitation is the neglecting through hurry of the necessary steps to make a proper decision. Inconsideration is the habitual neglect of important aspects of the problems to be solved. Inconstancy refers to the inability to stick to the good which has been decided on. Negligence means omitting to pay attention to what one should. Prudence of the flesh is a very serious fault, consisting in taking as one's ultimate end in life some good of the body; for instance, the development of a muscular physique or an enticing figure. Thus it would be contrary to prudence to be so solicitous about physical goods that our attention is detracted from higher pursuits. Our solicitude should be directed rather to the achieving of spiritual goods. We should not worry about the physical necessities we require, but merely make a normal, reasonable effort to get them and let it go at that. The same holds in regard to future contingencies. Everything should be taken care of in its proper time, so that it is imprudent to worry oneself about what can be taken care of only at a later time. What this means then is that we should use foresight and prepare for the future, but only to the extent that we can reasonably expect our efforts to succeed. A majority of the violations against prudence arise from the sense appetites. Sensual pleasures, especially those of sex, so attract and absorb our attention that they prevent the prudent evaluation of the situation.

QQ: 57-122: JUSTICE

Nature Of Justice

By justice we mean a habit by which we have a firm and constant will to render to everyone his right. Hence it is the function of justice to establish among men the proper order and to maintain it. In a general way then, inasmuch as they all serve the common good, every virtue can be said to be a form of justice, which in this broad sense is called legal justice. In its more common and restricted sense though, justice is a distinct virtue by which the interrelations of men are regulated, so that each one is given what is coming to him.

The Work Of Judges

The very etymology of the word indicates that the function of a judge is to define or determine what is just. To be licit, a judge's decisions must satisfy three conditions: they must result from a desire to do justice, they must be backed with the proper authority and they must be based upon prudent deliberation. It would then be unjust to condemn anyone merely on suspicion of wrongdoing. Moreover, since it is unjust to think poorly of anyone unless there is cogent proof to warrant it, a judge should always give the accused the benefit of the doubt whenever he can. To maintain justice, a judge should not try to change the laws, but should render judgment according to them, because real laws are simply declarations of the basic principles of right and justice.

Types Of Justice

Following Aristotle, Aquinas distinguishes two species of justice, the commutative and the distributive. The former is concerned with the regulation of the relations which private citizens have with each other. The latter is concerned with the proper distribution to its citizens by the community of the common burdens, advantages and honors. Like all moral virtues, justice lies in the golden mean; but, as Aristotle also says, this mean is according to a geometric proportion in distributive justice, but according to an arithmetic one in commutative justice. The typical case of commutative justice is found in buying and selling: the exchange should be of equivalents. But, according to distributive justice, people do not receive all the same, but often widely different, shares because they differ in their merits, status or capabilities. Thus, only the most worthy receive public honors, and all may be subject to taxes, but in varying amounts.

Restitution

Restitution is the contrary of taking away. So, since taking what is somebody else's is unjust, restitution, by which that unjust inequality is rectified, pertains to commutative justice. It is then wrong not to provide restitution for what one has unjustly taken. How much restitution should be provided can vary. It should be at least equal to what was taken but may be more, because a twofold injustice may be involved: the loss itself and the further damage resulting, say, from the violence employed to take it. Thus a judge will often order simple restitution plus punitive damages. Restitution should also be made immediately, because any delay compounds the original injustice.

Violations Of Commutative Justice

These consist mainly of what we may call respect of persons which is manifested in the distribution of goods, not on the proper basis of qualifications or worthiness, but because the receiver is a person who is a relative, friend or the like. Thus, in electing officials, citizens should be careful to vote for those whom they consider the best candidates. Likewise, respect for persons should be avoided in the dispensation of public honors and of justice in the courts.

Homicide

Turning to the violations of commutative justice, we may first consider murder. Not all killing is murder and wrong. Plants and brutes exist for the good of men, and so it is not wrong to kill them when necessary for some reasonable end. If, however, a man happens to be through his own fault a serious danger to the community, it is permissible for the common good to execute him, as the part is subordinate to the whole. To do this would not be right for any one, but only those in charge of the community. To kill oneself is evil for a threefold reason: it is contrary to the natural inclination we have to self-preservation and to the charity we should have for ourselves; it is an injustice to the community to which we belong; it is also a violation of God's right over our lives. It is clear than that under no condition should we ever kill an innocent person. If, however, someone is threatening our life or some important property, it is permissible to kill him if this is necessary.

Mutilation

A part always exists for the sake of the whole. What then is a proper handling of any part is relative to the good of the whole. If then any part of the body is healthy and performing its function, it would be contrary to the good of the whole to remove or mutilate it. On the other hand, if some section of the body is sick, it may be removed if this is necessary for the good of the whole body. Then too, insofar as each man is a part of the community, mutilation may be used as a punishment by the community if this is necessary to preserve order.

Punishment

Beating differs from mutilation, inasmuch as it only gives pain, whereas mutilation damages the integrity of the body. Although beating thus does much less harm to the body than mutilation, it would still be unjust to give one except as a punishment for some fault, and unless it is administered by a legal superior. Another licit way of punishing would be to deprive the evildoer of his freedom of movement or of the use of his body by imprisonment or shackling.

Violations Of Property

God made all the things of this world for the use of men. It is then natural for us to use them, but to do so effectively it is necessary that we have private property for three reasons. Men tend to work with the required care and industry only when they know the fruits of their labor will go to them. The orderly fulfilling of the needs of men can be achieved only when everyone looks out for himself. Order and peace in a community are much more easily maintained when every man has his own property. Private property is thus a natural right, but the particular rules to follow in regard to their acquisition and use must be determined by positive law. The natural law also requires, however, that each one use his property in a socially responsible way. Thus, we are required to share our goods with those who are in desperate need, unless we are in a similar condition. By theft we mean the covert taking of another's possessions. It is therefore a violation of justice. Robbery differs from simple theft in that it is the open and violent taking of the property of others. Note, however, that taking what belonged to others does not always constitute theft or robbery. For the goods of this world are for the use of all men. When a person is in dire and urgent need, and no other way of saving himself is available except by helping himself to the property of others, this is neither theft nor robbery since in such a case he has a right to such goods.

Injustice In The Courts

Since it is the precise function of the courts to maintain justice, numerous are the forms of injustice practiced in them. First, in regard to the judges themselves. Clearly, only duly authorized persons can serve as judges. Moreover, they must remain within their own jurisdiction. Then too, since a judge renders judgment as a public official, this requires that he base his judgment only on what he knows in his official capacity: the laws and the evidence presented. He cannot use information which he has as a private person. Justice also requires that no one be condemned unless he is first accused and given a chance to defend himself. But once a defendant has been proven guilty, the judge must condemn him in accord with the law. He cannot pardon him. Only the ruler of the state can do this if he judges it to be for the common good. Turning now to the functions of the prosecutor, we must keep in mind that his aim should be the punishment of evildoers, but also that punishments are not to be sought for their own sake. Because this life is only a time of probation, punishments should be basically medicinal, serving either to make the culprit a better person or the state more peaceful and orderly. A prosecutor must in justice seek convictions in all cases which involve violation of public order, and in which he can get enough evidence to make success likely.

It is also necessary, to maintain justice, that the accusation and proceedings be recorded in writing. Otherwise, stories would be changed and facts forgotten, to the detriment of equity. Obviously too, the charges should be made truthfully and promptly. In regard to the accused, he must answer truthfully whatever question is licitly put to him. However, although he should never lie, this does not mean that he has to tell everything he knows. He can often protect himself by not volunteering information which might be to his disadvantage, and this is licit. He would also do wrong to appeal his case when he knows he is guilty. In regard to witnesses, they should appear when required by the authorities or when it is necessary to prevent an injustice. For them to bear false testimony would be wrong on three counts: violation of their oath, injustice to the accused and untruthfulness.

Injustice Through Speech

This occurs in various ways. Contumely consists of using words or deeds intentionally to deprive another of his due honor. In its worse forms this can be a serious sin, because honor is as dear to most men as possessions. Backbiting, on the other hand, is the underhanded destruction of the reputation of another. In itself this is not as bad as murder, but is worse than theft. Note too that anyone who accepts a backbiter shares in his evil deed. Gossiping is very similar in many ways to backbiting, but they differ in their aim. The gossip intends to sow discord among friends, while the backbiter wants to destroy the reputation of others. Because friends are among the greatest goods that we have, gossiping is worse than both contumely and backbiting. Derision when done in jest may not be evil, but when done deliberately to make a person seem contemptible, it may be a serious sin. Cursing is either wishing or commanding that another be afflicted with some evil. To curse irrational things is wrong because it is silly. To curse a human is wrong because it is contrary to the charity we owe to all. The degree of its sinfulness depends on its circumstances.

Fraud

The purpose of buying and selling is the good of the parties involved, since each needs what the other has. Money has been invented to facilitate these exchanges, by making it easy to establish a price for various objects. Justice involves that the price of any object correspond to its real value. Fraud is the sale of an object for more than its just price. What a just price is, however, depends on a number of factors. Sometimes, for instance, because of sentimental reasons a just price might be higher than the mere intrinsic value. On the other hand, a seller should not try to raise his price to take advantage of the need of the buyer. Nor is the maxim "Let the buyer beware" a valid one. The just price of anything cannot therefore be determined down to the last penny. It is only estimated and can be known only as falling within a certain range. Fraud can be perpetrated in three ways: by selling one kind of thing for another or by giving the wrong quantity or quality. When done deliberately it is wrong and requires restitution. If done unintentionally it is not a sin but still requires restitution when discovered.

Religion

Justice manifest itself in the form of a number of subordinate virtues. One of the most important of these is religion, by which we render to God the honor due him. It expresses itself primarily in interior acts and secondarily in exterior ones. These are necessary not because God needs them, but for our own good. We can add nothing to God, but by extending to him reverence and honor we perfect ourselves, inasmuch as we are fulfilling the role for which we were made. One act of religion is prayer, in which we ask God for what we need. Many men have false notions about prayer. For instance, some think it is useless because God is immutable.

Others think prayers can make God change his mind. However, the only reason we pray is that we might by so doing merit what God has from all eternity willed to give us if we do pray. We should pray then for whatever is right for us to want. Prayers should not be so long as to be tedious but should be as frequent as necessary to maintain our devotion. Other acts required by religion are adoration, the explicit acknowledgement of God's supremacy; sacrifice, the offering to God of physical goods as an expression of our subjection and reverence; the support of the clergy; the taking of vows, promises freely made to God to perform good actions that one would not otherwise be obliged to do; and the taking of oaths, in which we call upon God to witness that we speak the truth.

Vices Opposed To Religion

Superstition is opposed to the virtue of religion as an excess, insofar as it is the rendering of a divine cult to a nondivine being or to God in a manner that is not proper. There are different species of superstition. One form consists of abusing religious practices, e.g., the way some people use medals. Idolatry is the rendering to a creature such as an idol the worship which should be rendered only to God. Divination is the attempt to uncover the future in a manner contrary to the will of God, for instance, by palm-reading. Magic in the strict sense of the word, which implies a pact with evil spirits, is yet another type of superstition. Other serious offenses against religion are perjury, sacrilege and simony.

Filial Piety And Obedience

Another special form of justice is piety, by which we mean showing the proper honor and reverence to our superiors and to those on whom we depend. Primarily then, we owe piety to God; secondarily, to our parents and relatives, to our country and fellow countrymen. In regard to our parents it requires not only that we show them reverence, but that we aid them whenever they happen to need it. In regard to those in positions of authority, it requires that we give them both honor and obedience. In our various groups, to maintain order and get things done it is necessary that those in charge direct the others, in line with the authority they have received from God. It follows then that they should be obeyed. However, obedience is not owed to our superiors in all things. If the orders of one go contrary to those of another, clearly we should obey the higher authority. Nor do we need to obey a superior who gives orders pertaining to matters outside of his jurisdiction. Thus children need not obey their parents in regard to whom they will marry.

Comment

What would Thomas have said of our contemporary phenomenon of civil disobedience? Presumably he would hold it to be justified under certain conditions, namely, those mentioned above plus those required for good order and by prudence. For instance, to prevent the growth of a general spirit of lawlessness, civil disobedience should be used as infrequently as possible - only where there is a serious wrong to be corrected and where the action will have some chance of success.

Gratitude

In justice we should have gratitude to everyone who has done anything for us, in proportion to the good they have rendered us. Just as in the conferring of a benefit, the attitude of the giver is quite distinct from his gift, so the affection of a grateful person is to be distinguished from the gift he gives in return. The former should be manifested immediately; the latter need not. Among friends especially, what is exchanged is not as important as the affection which it betokens. We must not be too hasty in judging another to be ungrateful, because a person may often be prevented through some reason unknown to us from manifesting his gratitude. Even if a person's ingratitude becomes worse as we continue to try to help him, the proper thing to do is to imitate God's loving kindness and understanding and not cease aiding him.

Vengeance

It might seem that vengeance is always wrong, because contrary to charity; but we must distinguish on the basis of the motives acted upon. If someone takes revenge simply to do evil in return for that received, this would indeed always be uncharitable and wrong. If, however, the intention is to punish the wrongdoer in order to achieve some good, for instance, his rehabilitation or the maintenance of order and justice, in such a case revenge is licit, as long as all the proper circumstances are present. But to make evil people do what is right we must threaten them with the loss of a good which is greater than what they would gain through their evil actions. These threats then must concern what men love the most: life, bodily comfort, liberty, physical possessions, social position and glory. Thus the punishments customarily imposed: death, lashing, imprisonment, banishment, fines and public humiliation are quite reasonable.

Truthfulness

Since man is a social animal he naturally owes to his fellows whatever is necessary for the maintenance of society. But social life is impossible unless men can believe each other. It therefore follows that truthfulness is another special form of justice. There are several vices opposed to truthfulness. One is mendaciousness or the habit of telling lies. To tell a lie consists basically in saying something we believe to be false. Thus, if we mistakenly think something to be false and say the opposite, what we say is true but we still lied. Most of the time people lie in order to deceive others, but we can lie even in cases where we know deception is impossible, as occurs when two diplomats swap lies with each other. Deception then and the intention to deceive are not of the essence of lying. We may distinguish three sorts of lies: the pernicious, in which we intend to harm the hearer: the jocose, which is said as a jest; and the officious, which is said in the hope of helping the listener, as when a doctor may tell a dying man that he still has a long time to live. Lying is wrong in itself because it is unnatural and improper to say what we think not to be true. However, it is not always a mortal sin. It may easily be so in the case of a pernicious lie because this is a direct violation of justice and charity. The contrary is usually the case with jocose and officious lies. But even these may be serious sins if scandal results. Another vice opposed to truthfulness is hypocrisy, trying to seem what we are not. There is a twofold evil here: first the lack of a certain virtue, then the simulation of it. If one wills both of these, it is a serious evil. If one wills only the second, it may be either a mortal or venial sin, depending on the circumstances. Also opposed to truthfulness is boasting, the extolling of oneself beyond measure. This can also be either a moral or venial sin depending on the circumstances.

Friendliness

The good of society requires that all men control both their speech and actions, so as to maintain reasonably smooth social relations. The habit of so acting we call friendliness, and it also is a form of justice since by it we render to our fellow men what is their due. The one who carries friendliness to excess is guilty of flattery. The opposite vice is quarrelsomeness.

Generosity

God gives to some more possessions than they need so that they might merit by sharing them as they should. For a person really needs little to live reasonably. To be generous within one's capacities is therefore praiseworthy and virtuous. Obviously, however, generosity does not mean giving away what one needs to support one's own family, which would be unjust. It refers rather to the rational use of one's superfluity to help others. Though strictly not a form of justice, it is related and complementary to it since it deals with our relations with others and with the proper use of physical goods. One vice opposed to generosity is covetousness, the excessive love of possessions. This is one of the capital vices because it leads to so many other sins: fraud, lying, perjury, discontent, violence and hardness of heart. The contrary vice is prodigality, careless and imprudent squandering.

Equity

Laws are necessarily general, dictating what should be usually done. They simply cannot serve as a guide for every individual case, because of the infinite variations and complications which arise in human affairs. To follow the laws literally in every case would often be contrary to justice and the common good, the ends which the laws were made to ensure. In such a situation it is necessary to make oneself cognizant of it, ignore the letter of the law and follow what is required by justice and the common good. This is the function of the virtue we call equity.

QQ. 123-140: FORTITUDE

Nature Of Fortitude

A virtue, we have seen, is a habit that makes a man be good and act well. The intellectual virtues perfect our cognitive activities. Justice establishes rectitude in our external relations. Fortitude and temperance are concerned with removing impediments to our acting rightly. Fortitude is the habit that does this by perfecting the irascible ("fighter") appetite and thus making us capable of resisting and overcoming the difficulties which arise in life and which tend to turn us away from what reason requires. These difficulties are impediments to right action because they cause us to fear them. By fortitude we repress such fears, but we also moderate any tendency to overaudaciousness, which would carry us to the opposite extreme.

Vices Opposed To Fortitude

A good man is one who lives a rationally ordered life, which in turn requires that our various appetites be ever subject to the reason. Reason dictates, however, that we flee some things and seek after others, in varying degrees. To fear the dangerous is reasonable and therefore no sin. But to flee what we ought to stand up to is due to an inordinate and therefore sinful fear, which we call cowardliness. Some people, however, are so overconfident or stupid that they fear nothing. Such insensibility is irrational and hence wrong too. A related vice is foolhardiness, the unreasonable rushing into dangers that could be avoided.

Virtues Associated With Fortitude

Magnanimity means literally "great of soul." It is a habit by which we tend to concern ourselves mainly with affairs of importance, while avoiding those that are incompatible with the quest for excellence. Opposed to it are the vices of presumption, by which we aspire to do more than we are capable of; overambitiousness; vainglory, by which we desire honors inordinately; and small-mindedness, by which we fail to live according to the fullness of our capabilities. Magnificence is a virtue by which we do grand things in proper style. As examples we could give the creation of the Parthenon or of the great Gothic cathedrals. Opposed to it are the vices of parsimony and vulgar extravagance. Other virtues connected with fortitude are patience, perseverance and constancy.

QQ. 141-170: TEMPERANCE

Nature Of Temperance

Just as fortitude perfects the irascible appetite, so does temperance perfect the concupiscible or pleasure appetite. The latter is a natural tendency to seek various pleasures. To allow it to function within the limits established by reason is good. However, the passions which flow from it are often strong and intractable. It is therefore necessary to develop a habit of rational control over them so that they will aid us in achieving our happiness rather than lead us into disastrous situations. Children often fall into the opposite vice of intemperance, unless they are well trained. Intemperance in adults is thus usually a consequence of the failure to mature normally. Although intemperance is in itself not as bad as many other vices, it is the most disgraceful because it lowers a man to the level of the brutes.

Species

There are different species of temperance, depending on which actions are to be controlled. Since the actions which produce the most physical pleasure are those connected with food, drink and sex, the main types of temperance are distinguished accordingly. Abstinence is the virtue by which we eat only proper foods in proper quantities. Sometimes abstinence requires that we fast, that is, that we do without food for a certain time. This is necessary to help control physical desires and to enable the mind to think more clearly. We should fast especially from meat, eggs and milk foods, because these give the most pleasure, and they also tend to increase libidinous desires. Gluttony is the vice opposed to abstinence. Sobriety is the virtue by which we are temperate in our use of intoxicating drinks. The use of liquor is not in itself immoral. Indeed, the moderate use of it is helpful in many ways. But even a slightly excessive use is wrong as it deprives us of the use of reason. Sobriety is especially required in those who have tendencies to overdrink, in the young who are just learning how to control themselves, in women since they do not have enough strength of character to resist the lure of pleasure and in people who have positions of responsibility which demand clear heads. Obviously, drunkenness is the contrary vice. Chastity is the virtue by which we regulate our sexual life in a rational way. To determine what is and is not rational we must consider the purpose of sex. Clearly, it is to ensure the preservation of the species. The rational use of it then requires that it be for this end and under the proper conditions (e.g., marriage) and in the proper manner.

Comment

Thomas' remark on the aphrodisiacal nature of some foods does not seem to square with our experience of them, but obviously would apply to any that were such. In his views on women, we suspect he fell prey to a prejudice of his time. In regard to the purpose of sex, it would seem an oversimplification to consider only its biological aim, as he does here.

Impurity

Impurity is the vice opposed to chastity. It takes a number of different forms. Fornication is sexual intercourse between unmarried people. This is a serious sin because it makes it very difficult for the ensuing children to be raised properly. It would follow then that any actions, such as kissing, when they incite one to impurity, are also grievously wrong. Other forms of impurity are seduction, rape, adultery, incest, masturbation, bestiality and homosexuality. Of these, the last three are the worst, because they are unnatural.

QQ. 179-189: STATES OF LIFE

The Contemplative Life

Every living being manifests its nature by performing the actions proper to it. Men do this especially by thinking and acting in accord with reason. Some prefer the former and some, the latter. As a result we can distinguish two main types of life, the contemplative and the active. Those who are concerned principally with the seeking of knowledge are said to live contemplative lives. This does not mean that they are without feelings, as the reason they contemplate is that they love truth and so have the highest pleasure when they possess it. The intellectual virtues are thus essential to the contemplative life, but the moral virtues are only necessary to it in order to maintain the proper dispositions. Its ultimate perfection consists in the very act of contemplating the truth, but we achieve this only through a number of other acts: the understanding of various facts and principles and the deduction from them of further truths. We learn in various ways: through prayer, discussing with others, reading and meditation. The main object of our contemplation is necessarily the divine truth, which in the future life we shall know perfectly. In the present life, however, since we can attain only to a most imperfect knowledge of God, we must study in detail the universe which as his effect can bring us to some knowledge of him.

The Active Life

The active life is concerned with doing things, and so the moral virtues pertain essentially to it; and it will not continue when we leave this world. Comparing the active with the contemplative life, we find that in itself the contemplative is far superior. It perfects the intellect, which is the highest faculty in us, can function over longer periods of time, gives greater pleasure, has fewer exterior requirements, is more desirable in itself and makes us more similar to God. Nevertheless, in some situations it may be preferable to adopt an active life because of the press of immediate needs. It likewise follows that the contemplative life is in itself the more meritorious, but in individual cases an activist can merit more than a contemplative if, for instance, he develops a greater charity whereby for some worthy purpose he foregoes the immediate satisfactions of contemplation. In one sense, it is obvious that the active life is an impediment to the contemplative, because you cannot lead both together. From another point of view, it is no impediment but rather a requirement, because before one can achieve the contemplative life, he must establish himself in the world and learn to control himself.

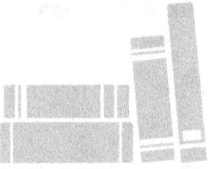

ON KINGSHIP

INTRODUCTION

In conclusion we shall consider briefly a short pamphlet, *On Kingship*, composed in the 1260's. Aquinas apparently wrote it as a gift for a friend who was king of Cyprus. It is divided into four books, of which probably only the first and chapters one to four of the second are authentic. There is, however, nothing unthomistic in the remainder. The work is interesting and of value because it is the only one which Thomas formally and from a personal point of view treats of the philosophy of the state. True, he had commented on Aristotle's Politics, but there he was interested only, as a commentator should, in explaining what the author meant. Even though he may have agreed with Aristotle for the most part, we know that he did, not from the commentary, but from such a personal work as *On Kingship*. His aim in writing it was simple: to describe how governments started and what the functions of the rulers were. While many of his points are obviously dated, his basic ideas would still muster considerable support. We must remember too that in writing it he was trying to show a medieval prince what kind of ruler he should be.

NATURE OF THE STATE

Man is by nature a social and political animal. This is clear from the fact that nature provides the brutes with food, dress and means of defense, but it has given man reason by which he can acquire all these things, but only with the help of many others. Then too, the brutes have innate knowledge of whatever they need to know, but men do not, so each has to specialize in a given area and contribute to the general fund of knowledge whatever few truths he might discover. This is one reason too why only men have developed languages. Thus is it by their very nature necessary for men to live in society. It is then by an equally natural necessity that men form states, that is, that they establish instruments to maintain peace and order. When many men live together, each seeking his own advancement, the result can only be chaos unless there is someone who has charge of ensuring the common good. A state then is good if ruled for the benefit of the whole. It is bad if ruled for the private benefit of the rulers. We can then distinguish three types of just and three types of unjust states. Among the latter, a tyranny is the rule by one man for his own personal ends; an oligarchy is the rule of a few rich to exploit the many; a "democracy" is the exercise of power by the multitude at the expense of the rich. Among the just states, a "polity" is ruled by the masses; an aristocracy, by a virtuous few; a monarchy, by one man.

MONARCHY THE BEST

To decide which of the just forms of government is the best we must determine which achieves its end the most efficiently. Now the end of any just state is to maintain unity and peace. It is obvious that unity can be better achieved under one man than many; so, monarchy is the best form of government. We might adduce several reasons for this. When many rule, they must establish a unity among themselves; the king does not have to. If a state is to achieve a high level of efficiency and unity such as is found in nature objects, it must be organized in a similar manner; but in all natural objects control is centered in one of the parts. Experience shows too that countries without kings are rent with dissensions, whereas those under one ruler enjoy peace, justice and prosperity. But just as monarchy is the best form of government, so is tyranny the worst. The reason is clear enough. One-man rule being the most efficient, if the ruler is a scoundrel he can do much more harm.

THE NATURE OF KINGSHIP

We can best understand what being a ruler involves by considering how natural objects are ruled, for instance, the whole universe by God or man by the soul. Indeed, there is quite an analogy between the universe, a man and a realm. In each case there is a multitude of parts which are all governed by one ruler. By looking at what God does, we can see what a king should do. Now, God does two things. He sets up the world and he also rules it after he has set it up. Few kings have to set up their own states, but they all have to rule. Nevertheless, both are kingly functions, but in the case of a human king he has to use what already pre-exists in nature. How he orders these, however, depends on the end to be achieved. But the reason men form states is not just to live but to live well. In turn, to live a full life in this world is not an end desired for itself, but only a means to achieving union with God in the next. This then is also the ultimate end of the state, and everything that the king does should be ordered to it. In other words, the state exists to make it possible for men to live virtuous lives and thus prepare themselves for an eternity of bliss with God. It is therefore the function of the king to establish and maintain an order that will tend to ensure a good and virtuous life for all the citizens. This common good presents two different aspects. The main one is the virtuous life of the citizens. The secondary one is the development of the physical goods required for a virtuous life. It is then up to the king to take positive action to maintain peace and order, to direct his subjects along the proper, virtuous lines of action and to ensure prosperity.

SPECIFIC DUTIES OF KINGS

To attain these main ends the king has to take care of a number of subordinate matters. He has to replace his officials as they get old or die, to enforce the laws so that by proper rewards and punishments his subjects will be led to avoid iniquity and to live virtuously, protect the country against its enemies, choose the most advantageous sites for forts, cities, colonies and so forth, to develop the agricultural resources so as to make each part of the realm as self-sufficient as possible, to encourage the growth of flocks and herds, to mint enough money to satisfy all the financial needs of the realm, to establish strong lines of defense, to connect all parts of the country with roads and maintain security on them, to establish a system of weights and measures so that trade and industry will be facilitated, to provide for the needy out of the public treasury and, finally, to support the public worship of God.

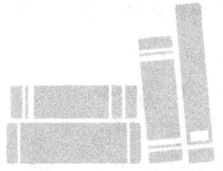

ESSAY QUESTIONS AND ANSWERS

Question: What influence has the philosophy of Aquinas had since his death?

Answer: Many of his contemporaries considered Thomas a dangerous radical and they opposed to his views the traditional Augustinian philosophy. Thus, though he had many followers even when still alive, his theories were far from receiving general acceptance. After his death this continued to be the case. Many thinkers, especially among the Dominicans, rallied to his philosophy, but several new and powerful antagonists also took to the field. In the generation after Thomas, there was John Duns Scotus, whose blend of Aristotelian and Augustinian ideas with his own laid the basis of the Scotistic school of thought, which continued till the end of the Middle Ages to be perhaps as influential as the Thomistic. In the fifteenth century, however, neither of these schools had as many adherents as the "nominalism" of William of Ockham (1290-1350). One of the main reasons why Thomism never became the dominant philosophy seems to be that even among his most devoted followers very few understood his basic notion of existence as the fundamental act of all things. As a result most of them explained his distinction between quiddity and existence as though they were two things, which is not only untenable but absurd.

At the beginning of the modern period the teaching of philosophy in the universities had dropped pretty low. The dominant Ockhamism was basically skeptical; the Scotists were known primarily for the subtlety of their distinctions; Thomism was taught in a form that was a caricature. As a result there was a widespread reaction against all medieval philosophy, and new philosophers sought to provide a more useful and adequate replacement. Among them were Bacon, Hobbes, Locke, Descartes and Leibniz. These new systems, and those that came after them, gained widespread support and to a large degree supplanted the scholastic philosophies in the universities. Thomism continued to be studied, especially in Catholic countries and even more in Catholic seminaries, but from secondary sources which presented it in a highly corrupt form, at first with ideas from Francis Suarez (1548-1617), an early Jesuit philosopher; later on with ideas from Descartes, Locke and Leibniz. In the nineteenth century a slew of idealist and materialist philosophies made their appearance and dominated the intellectual life. However, their relativism and subjectivism seemed untenable to many people. A few of these, in the hope of finding a more solid philosophy, started to study the texts of the great medieval philosophers of the thirteenth century. They found that these men had long been misinterpreted and misunderstood and that, moreover, many of their answers to philosophical problems made much more sense than those of later thinkers. This seemed to be especially true of the views of Aquinas. This renewal of interest in Thomas spurted forward with the support given it in 1879 by Pope Leo XIII, who urged all who sought the truth to study Aquinas and to base their views on his, while correcting him wherever modern discoveries show it to be necessary. Since then numerous scholars have specialized in the history of medieval philosophy. They have done away with the accretions of centuries of misunderstanding, so that today medieval philosophy is understood better than ever before.

Another result is that Thomism has been accepted so widely that it is today followed by perhaps more people than any other system. There is no doubt that the adoption of Thomism by the Catholic Church as its official philosophy has been a factor in this development, but many Catholics reject Thomism while many non-Catholics have embraced it.

Question: Of what importance is the notion of participation in the philosophy of Aquinas?

Answer: Although Aquinas nowhere gives an extended discussion of his views on participation, he is continually speaking of it in passing and it is one of his basic notions. The idea is found even in Parmenides, but Plato among the ancients perhaps made most use of it. For him the Ideas, the pure, self-subsistent essences of all things, existed eternally and immutably in their own realm, which is different from our world. They were the archetypes of the things of this world, which are therefore said to participate in the Ideas, since they are made to be the kind of things they are by sharing in the universal essence. According to Plato, the cause of this participation is a God-like being he called the Demiurge, who produces things by using the Ideas as patterns. St. Augustine modified the Platonic theory by explaining the production of the world through its creation by God, who patterned things, not on Ideas existing eternally outside of himself, but on his own eternal ideas. Aquinas adopted the view of Augustine but extended it considerably. Things are not only participations in the divine ideas, but they are also participations in the divine existence. God is the pure act of being and so he participates in no other thing, whereas every other thing that exists does only insofar as God has willed it to share in the fullness of his being. Participation then is a kind of sharing, but it differs from the usual type of physical sharing that we are familiar with. In the latter case, for instance, if people share a pie, their sharing in the pie destroys it. In sharing by participation, however, what is shared in is not destroyed but may on the contrary be enriched. Nor are we by participating in God's existence made a part of him physically. We are all distinct from God. Yet we are only because he has willed us to be. Thus, though we are essentially different from him we are similar to him to a slight extent insofar as we all exist, though in ways that are very different. In this way the theory of participation provides the solution to the perennial problem of "the one and the many." All things are one insofar as they exist and exist through participation in a unique source. They are many insofar as they participate in varying degrees in the fullness of being.

Question: What is the central characteristic theory of Thomistic philosophy?

Answer: Thomas never indicated what he himself considered to be his most central and characteristic theory, so we have to try to figure it out for ourselves. Different scholars have defended a number of interpretations. Among the ideas suggested have been those of being, order, participation and the theory of act and potency. We suspect that the disagreement is for the most merely a verbal one. The basic position of Thomistic philosophy can be expressed in terms of any of these theories, but in every case the other theories are implied and necessarily involved. As an example let us take the view that emphasizes order. The whole universe manifests itself to us as one magnificent order. It consists of an indefinitely great number of substances, each one related to the others in a number of different ways: spatially, temporally and so forth. Above all, however, they are related teleologically. Each one has certain objective ends as a result of which it is subordinated to some and is superior to certain others. To achieve these ends they each have their own **metaphysical** structure. As a further result, all things interact more or less immediately with everything else. Such an order implies a supremely intelligent source who is also infinite, omnipotent and the pure act of existence. The order he has established can be understood by men, whom he has endowed with intelligence and freedom. Men are not only a part of the cosmic order; they also help to make it what it is. Men create societies and cultures which transform the face of the earth, which change men themselves, and today we are on the verge of extending this dominion even to the other planets. But the cosmic and social orders have their analogues in every individual substance and even in every atom. In each of them we find subordination and interrelation of parts.

But to understand this order and how it came about, the theory of actuality and potentiality is essential. For God can be the source of the universe only insofar as he is pure actuality. His creatures cannot be pure act like him, but are necessarily composed of act and potency. The degree of actuality they have determines their place and function in the cosmic order. We also, however, need the notion of participation which illuminates, for instance, the relationship between God and the various genera and species of things he has created. The notion of being is also basic. For all things are beings. God is the pure act of being, and all creatures participate in God's being. But in God essence is identical with existence, whereas in creatures there is a real distinction between the two.

Question: What are some of the major differences between Thomistic philosophy and its rival schools of modern philosophy?

Answer: Idealists, like Hegel, hold that reality is at bottom mental: what we call material has no existence independently of the thinking mind but is only an idea of that mind. Logical positivists are a type of materialist: they hold that mind and mental phenomena are reducible to matter, which is thus the basic stuff of the universe. Both idealists and materialists are monistic: they hold all reality to consist ultimately of only one kind of being. Thomists, however, are dualists. They hold that parts of the real are material and others are mental or spiritual, and that these two categories are ultimate, irreducible one to the other. Many idealists are pantheists; they hold that everything is a part of God; they usually maintain too that God is not free, that his nature necessitates him to do whatever he does in just the way that he does it. The materialists simply reject the possibility of any deity. Thomists, however, hold that we can demonstrate that there is a God, that he is distinct from all the rest of the universe and that he is to supereminent degree a person: he is supremely intelligent and free. Materialists of different sorts, like Freud, Dewey and John Watson, consider man to be merely a highly developed animal, that therefore cannot be said to be spiritual or immortal. For idealist personalists, like B. P. Bowne, man is essentially a person, a non-physical, immortal, rational and free being. For Thomists man is without doubt an animal with a physical body, but he is also a spiritual soul which is immortal. For materialists, thinking is a highly complicated function of the brain which is basically very similar to what a computer does, and which is therefore reducible to the interaction of physical particles and forces. For the idealist personalists, thinking is a purely spiritual activity which we perform as the result of the interaction which takes place between the divine and all human minds. The Thomists recognize two forms of knowledge: sensation, which takes place when sense organs are stimulated by exterior or interior causes, and thinking, which is a spiritual activity in which the data provided by sensation are used to arrive at universal concepts, which can then be combined to form judgments, which in turn are combined in reasonings. Because they hold man to be only a physical being, most materialistists maintain, quite consistently, that he is then not free, but subject to universal laws which describe how he is in all cases determined to act. Thomists, along with many idealists, hold that experience makes it clear that man is determined in some of his actions and is always influenced to a greater or lesser degree by various outside factors, in whatever he does; but experience also shows that men are very often not determined in making their choices but are free. For the materialists, man is just a relatively insignificant conglomeration of atoms which lasts for a certain period of time and then is dissolved. Idealists and Thomists hold that as free and intelligent beings men have a destiny which far transcends their physical existence. In regard to what constitutes good and evil, the pragmatists would say that whatever solves our problems to our satisfaction is good; what does not, is evil. The "Playboy" philosophy holds that whatever satisfies our instinctual cravings, especially our sexual ones, is good; whatever interferes with their satisfaction is evil. Thomists maintain that to be good, actions have to be in accord with the ends and nature of the universe and man.

Question: How would Thomism explain and defend basic human rights and dignity?

Answer: According to the Thomistic philosophy of life, God created men rational and free, so that we can freely cooperate with him in achieving the ends for which he made the world. But to attain these ends we need various goods: life, health, food, relaxation, education and so forth. These goods and the claim we therefore have to them are both called rights. We have such rights then because we are free, and we are made to attain certain ends. These rights are ours because of our very nature and so are inalienable. They may be guaranteed by civil laws but are prior to them and to the civil rights by which they may be supplemented. The fact that we are persons, and thus are of all creatures of this world the most similar to God and called to the most sublime end, gives each one of us an intrinsic value and dignity far above that of any animal or thing. We should then treat every human with the proper respect, observing all his rights and seeking to extend to him all possible understanding, sympathy and charity, no matter what his race, color, creed or age.

BIBLIOGRAPHY

WORKS OF AQUINAS

Basic Writings of Saint Thomas Aquinas, edited by A. Pegis. 2 vols. New York, Random House, 1944. Convenient and lengthy selections.

Summa Theologiae. Latin text and English translation, Introductions, Notes, Appendices and Glossaries. 60 vols. New York, McGraw-Hill, 1964. Translations are often rather free. Explanatory material is useful.

On the Truth of the Catholic Faith (Summa Contra Gentiles). 5 vols. Garden City, Hanover House, 1954-6. Also available in paperback.

GENERAL WORKS ON AQUINAS AND HIS PHILOSOPHY

Bourke, V. *Aquinas' Search for Wisdom.* Milwaukee, Bruce, 1965. An up-to-date, complete and readable account of Aquinas' life and work.

Chesterton, G. K. *St. Thomas Aquinas.* London, Hodder & Stoughton, 1947. Especially good for its treatment of Aquinas' intellectual and cultural background.

Gilson, E. *Being and Some Philosophers*. Toronto, Pontifical Institute of Mediaeval Studies, 1949. Compares Thomas' notion of being with those of the major philosophers. Sometimes difficult but most rewarding.

Gilson, E. *The Christian Philosophy of Saint Thomas Aquinas*. New York, Random House, 1956. A detailed and scholarly introduction to the thought of Aquinas.

Gilson, E. *The Elements of Christian Philosophy*. New York, New American Library, 1960. A brief introduction to the main ideas of Aquinas.

Gilson, E. *The Spirit of Mediaeval Philosophy*. New York, Scribner's, 1940. A classic introduction to the philosophy of the Middle Ages.

Garrigou-Lagrange, R. *Reality, a Synthesis of Thomistic Thought*. St. Louis, Herder, 1950. A helpful introduction to the theology and philosophy of Aquinas.

Meyer, H. *The Philosophy of St. Thomas Aquinas*. St. Louis, Herder, 1948. A recent systematization of the philosophy of Aquinas.

Phillips, R. P. *Modern Thomistic Philosophy*. 2 vols. Westminster, Md., Newman, 1950. Typical contemporary systematization of Aquinas' philosophy.

DICTIONARIES

Wuellner, B. *Dictionary of Scholastic Philosophy*. Milwaukee, Bruce, 1956. Useful because even unabridged dictionaries often do not explain the precise meaning of scholastic technical terms.

www.ingramcontent.com/pod-product-compliance
Lightning Source LLC
LaVergne TN
LVHW011708060526
838200LV00051B/2816